ALL IN A FAMILY

ALL IN A FAMILY

by Michael Gaydos

And Friends

New Leaf Press
P.O. BOX 311, GREEN FOREST, AR 72638

First Printing, April, 1977
Second Printing, February, 1987

Library of Congress Catalog Card Number: 76-5-2279
International Standard Book Number: 0-89221-029-x

Lovingly dedicated to the family of God with deep affection and the Lord's blessing.

Beloved Father Arthur
Tom and Nancy Adams and Family
Deacon Ken and Ann Bates
Don and Alberta Beckman
Tom and Donna Brennan
Michael and Jane Brown and Family
Al and Lorraine Carlson
In Memory of Dolores Carlson
Doctor John Cesnik and Family
Joseph and Emily Cisek
Rosemary Coyle
Tom and Olga Decerbo
Denny and Petie Dinsimore
The Cliff Dudley Family
Steve and Norma Eisner
Doctor Daniel Fink and Staff
Glenn and Carol Gilbert and Family
Doctor Marvin and Jan Halgrin
Holy Spirit Monastery
Tony and Shirley Istanish
Doctor and Mrs. Kaball
Philip and Mary Kerick
Doctor Ralph Lazzaro and Staff
Father John Lubey
The Locks
Manresa Retreat House
Rich and Pam Massanillo and Girls
Bishop John King Mussio
Jay McCaffery
Poor Clare Sisters and Monastery
Ed and Ione Puntsack and Family
Saint Regis Rectory
Resurrection Fellowship
Joe and Jan Robinson
My Beloved Son John
Doctor Sue and Family
Margaret Theisen
Bill and Mary White and Sons
Bernie Wesenberg
Doctor Gerald Stubbs and Family
McNeal Family

CONTENTS

AUTHOR'S INTRODUCTION

I was in my study praying, "Lord, what is it that you would have me to do as a Christian and a citizen of these United States during this year?

He impressed me to do two things: "Michael, travel from coast to coast to proclaim the gospel as you have in the past six years. Secondly, write a book on the healing of marriages and the restoration of the home and family."

I responded, "Lord, I am single. Why is it that you would have me write a book on family life?" The Lord said, "Michael, you have been a son and lived in a home and have been part of a family all of your life, and you have also had the distinct opportunity and privilege of living with many different kinds of families during your years of travel in the ministry.

"You have observed, experienced and learned much by living with these families. You have also gained much insight and made observations of all kinds of families—Catholic and Protestant, large and small; families where the fathers earn their living in varied occupations and professions, families that are very young and families that are much more mature and established. As you have lived in these homes, there has been an exchange. You have poured your life into those families by way of encouragement, love, teaching, ministering and prayer. They, in turn, have given much of their lives to you. They offer you love, affection, encouragement, prayer and strength when you have been weak and discouraged. Some have very liberally given to you financially to help you in your work. Others have offered you guidance and counsel, still others have given you legal and spiritual advice; and without their support, prayer and love, it would be impossible for you to minister and travel to the degree that you have.

"Michael, I have used these families to shape you and to

mold you. Share with the readers what you have learned and experienced, that they too may be blessed and their faith strengthened—that their vision will be expanded in seeing what I am doing around the nation and across the seas."

As I reflected on the word, it seemed to me the Lord wanted the readers to also see the vastness, beauty and loveliness of the body of Christ, and how great is the family of God. They may also see and know what it is to have brothers and sisters in Christ Jesus. And that I should share what I have learned that other families may be encouraged to grow strong in the faith.

Hanging in my den is a beautiful plaque that I purchased from Abbey Press. On it are engraved the following words:

If there is beauty in the character,
There will be harmony in the home.

If there is harmony in the home,
There will be order in the nation.

If there is order in the nation,
There will be peace in the world.

Certainly the enemy Satan has done much in recent decades to try to destroy the home. Families have been splintered and broken—going their various ways and each family member doing his own thing. There is little communication, dialogue, or very little understanding and exchange of love between its members.

During the past years of ministry, I have witnessed many divine healings. Certainly the Lord is healing the physical body, and He always has, since He is the same yesterday, and today, and forever. I have seen many of these healings and miracles taking place, particularly in the eyes, since the Lord has healed my eyes after wearing glasses for 30 years. It is clearly apparent that in this present day the Lord is doing so much in healing and restoring the home.

I have lived with many families that are indeed very

precious and beautiful. As these families began to share with me I soon realized that they had not always been that way. Somewhere along the line they had an experience—an encounter with Jesus and the power of the Holy Spirit. Because of this experience with the Lord, their personal lives and their homes have undergone radical changes for the better.

Before the Lord had called me into the ministry of evangelism in 1970, I had spent ten years in college, seminaries and universities studying. I also had the privilege of teaching in parochial elementary and secondary schools and on the junior college level. In addition, I have worked in summer-camp settings for most of the years that I was in school.

During all these years of formal training, I studied and learned a great deal of theory. This indeed has been helpful in my work. The important thing, however, does this apply to the "nitty-gritty" situation in the arena of life and day-to-day living? Also, is the teaching of the Word of God practical and applicable to family life?

Most important in this book is the "practical application" of Christianity to family life.

As I read the New Testament, it is very clear that Christianity was never intended to be a spectator sport. A spectator sport has been described as 22,000 people in the grandstands of a football game who are badly in need of exercise, watching 22 men on the field who are badly in need of rest. It can be observed that in some churches people gather to hear a choir sing, listen to a minister preach, or watch a priest stand at the altar celebrating the liturgy of the Eucharist. They sit watching and listening to what is taking place or being said. What is exciting to me is to see how people are really becoming involved in actively living and sharing their faith. The church is the body of believers—*Ecclesia,* the ones called out.

As I travel, I see the church, the body of believers, actively engaged in ministry. It is because of this that I have invited families that I have lived with and been a part of, to share their lives with you. They will share those things that they are learning and experiencing—their blessings, their victories in the Lord, as well as their failures, trials and difficulties.

We know that whatever maturity we do experience does not come overnight, but rather through years of growing and experiencing life.

I have invited each of these families to write on a different aspect of Christian life so that each chapter will be uniquely different in both subject matter and treatment. I have written an introduction to each chapter sharing with you how I know the family, as well as a few of my own thoughts and ideas on the topic being presented.

I would encourage you to share this book with your own family members as well as other families within your church or community. This, I believe, will bring you together. Another way of enjoying it would be to have a group rap session or dialogue—evaluating and exploring areas in your marriage or home that needs healing or improvement. Perhaps one family's strength will be another's weakness.

I believe most consider themselves to be part of an average American family, or a "good family," and most are; but as Christians, I don't think we should be satisfied with anything less than the very best that God intends us to have, to know, and to experience in Him.

One of the purposes of this book is that broken, wounded and divided families will find hope, faith, healing and unity. Also, that the good family, the average family, will be challenged to be even better; and lastly, that a really fine family will be challenged to be the best family possible in Christ.

An individual Christian life is a powerful witness to the world of the reality of Christ, but I believe a family that has it "together" as a family, is even a greater witness and testimony.

Those sharing couples sharing in the book, as well as

myself, do not think that we have "arrived" in the areas that we are discussing, or that we are perfect and have all the answers; but rather we are growing, we are exploring, we are endeavoring to respond to and live out the revelation of the Gospel in our lives and the directives of the Holy Spirit in guiding our steps day by day.

We would invite you to consider, share and explore with us how the Lord is perfecting the family. Take a "peek" into our hearts, our homes, and our lives. As we share, we may rejoice when our brother rejoices, and weep when he weeps. We may learn from others' mistakes and values, and rejoice in the blessings and miracles that God has brought to pass in our lives and in your life as well.

I am very grateful to Father Michael Scanlan, Father George Stockhowe and Cliff Dudley for their editorial advice and assistance; to my cousin, Joanne Scala, for her typing and encouragement, and acting as my secretary; and to Hilda Tarquinio and Madeline Estafen for their interest and assistance.

DAUGHTERS—BLESSINGS OR BRATS?

When I am ministering in Los Angeles, I stay with Attorney Richard Reinjohn and his family.   One day during my visit, his wife Ann came to the den and said, "Michael, there are some friends whom I would like for you to meet." I followed her to the living room and was introduced to Al and Georgia Ridgeway. I extended my hand and as they shook it, they looked at me as if I were Pope John, Oral Roberts and Pat Robertson all rolled into one.

Satan would want me to be swollen with pride when I am flattered, loved and admired; however, I have come to realize that when people do express their adulation and respect they are really loving Jesus in me.

Al and Georgia presented me with a very lovely gift on that day, and again the Lord brought two people into my life that would serve as one continued blessing of encouragement, prayer and support.

During my ministry in California, Al spent numerous evenings chauffering me to the various churches where I would be sharing. During this time we had the opportunity to get to know each other better.

Georgia's ministry to me has been letter writing. Hardly a week would go by without my receiving a letter from the

Ridgeways, no matter where I was in the country. Always these letters were uplifting and edifying; however, my busy traveling schedule often made it difficult to answer Georgia's correspondence.

It is my policy that anytime I receive a letter from anyone, I always acknowledge it. There is an old saying, "Write a letter to a busy person and you will be sure to get an answer." I have tried to make that adage a reality in my own personal life.

When thinking about doing this book, I knew it would be no trouble for the Ridgeways to contribute a chapter. Georgia is one of eight daughters, and now has four daughters of her own. In family life, there is a definite need for communication between parents and children. This chapter deals more specifically with the communication between mothers and daughters.

* * * * *

Hi! We're the Ridgeway girls: Rochelle, 17; Michelle, 15; Wendy, 12 and Jackie, 10. Our family decided on a few subjects and we've commented on them in the following pages. Hope they will help or encourage both parents and daughters. We love you.

ADVICE TO PARENTS BY DAUGHTERS

Rochelle: Realize that your children are getting older and they do go through many stages. Let your kids know that you do love them. You should always make sure that you discipline them for whatever wrong they might do. It proves to them that you care. They will understand as they get older.

Wendy: Be calm and patient with your daughter. Try not to get mad at her. Show her that you love her. Don't embarrass her in front of her friends.

ADVICE TO DAUGHTERS

Rochelle: All sisters need to depend on each other for various reasons. Do try to be helpful and understand each other. Before you know it you're all off on your own and there are so many things you wish could have been said or done.

Wendy: Obey your parents. Try to help out. Try not to get them mad at you. Don't talk back or yell at them.

PRAYER AT NIGHT

Rochelle: When my mother or father come and pray with us at night it is sort of a security feeling. They pray for good rest, our needs and for other people.

Michelle: I think it helps a lot because it gives me confidence in myself and God, and makes me feel better.

Wendy: It helps when someone else is praying with you. It makes you feel better and sleep better. It helps you not to forget to pray also.

Jackie: I like it because the next day seems to go better. We can pray for sick people that we hear about during the day, and they get well.

PRAYER FOR HURTS AND FEARS

Rochelle: We've always prayed for hurts and fears. Fears have been the biggest problem from when I was young until now. Some are just about growing up, fears of monsters or being alone. When you pray for your fears and you believe in what you prayed for, a kind of peace comes over you. Now, more than before, our family prays for hurts, not only physical but mental. Many people usually never think God would heal you in any way, but He does if you believe! Satan may try to interfere but he can't because we're God's children and God's strength overpowers Satan's.

Michelle: Sometimes it doesn't take the hurt away but that's because I'm so mad at it that I don't have enough faith for it to be healed.

Wendy: It helps when you think that if you die you'll go to heaven and that's better than being on this earth. If you get hurt you'll either die or get over it.

Jackie: I like it because prayer works.

PRAYER IN THE MORNING

Rochelle: I've never made it a habit to pray in the morning. I've just always prayed all through the day. Sometimes in the morning I may wake up and say "Thank You, Jesus, for everything." It does help your day. Anytime you think of it thank Jesus for anything.

Michelle: I usually pray to myself in the morning but it helps more when Mom prays for me. *(She asks for it often, Mom's note.)*

Wendy: I can't say it doesn't work, but the only way it helps that I see is that things don't go wrong, but doesn't always make your day extra special.

Jackie: Usually we're in a hurry and there isn't time. Maybe we should get up a few minutes earlier. It would probably help us.

NON–CHRISTIAN FRIENDS VISITING

Rochelle: I love making friends and we have always lived in a Christian atmosphere, neighborwise. Most of my friends now aren't strong Christians but do believe in Jesus. They are not really a bad influence on me. It just depends on how strong your beliefs are.

Michelle: It doesn't really bother me until I think they won't be going the same place I'll be going.

Wendy: It sort of bothers them when we pray aloud, except when we say grace at meals. We don't rush them into being a Christian because that might scare them. So we do it slowly.

16

SHARING JESUS

Rochelle: I love it.

Michelle: I like it. I think everyone should share their beliefs.

Jackie: (Mom is commenting for her.) "Jackie has been sharing Jesus with friends for years. Two years ago she was telling her Jewish friend all about Jesus and that she had to believe in Him to go to heaven."

DISCIPLINE

Rochelle: All of my life I've been disciplined. I see nothing wrong with it. I'm sure it helped me understand more through life. I know many kids who haven't been disciplined and they have much growing up to do.

Michelle: I don't like it! Everyone says it is for your own good but I haven't gotten any good out of it yet. I think there should be discipline but for a good reason.

Wendy: It depends on what you do. If you do something little and are disciplined for something big that's not fair.

Jackie: I don't like it, but God said we must have it or we'll turn into brats.

SHARING HURTS

Rochelle: I'm a complainer, everyone is apt to know what's wrong with me. I cry a lot and get hurt easily. I think it does help sharing your hurts. Someone may pray for you if you haven't been prayed for already. Plus, it gets it all out of you, like a release.

Michelle: I like it but sometimes when other people share it sounds phony.

Wendy: It's better talking over your problems and praying about them with someone. Then they're usually solved and gone.

COMMUNICATION WITH PARENTS

Rochelle: I have the best communication with my parents. They are very understanding and we get along great. Besides the help of being Christians, they understand. In growing up, my interests are constantly changing. I love to get out and keep busy. Communication with my parents means so much, it has a great deal to do with growing up. I love parties and would go every Friday and Saturday night. My mom would tell me, "Oh! you're going to get older and you'll be tired of parties and be bored." "Not me, I'd never get bored at parties," I'd say. I don't know if they have changed but, yes, I am bored with them. Many incidents like this happen. As we grow older we realize that what our parents have been telling us is true. Yet they realize also the things I want and have to do.

I think being the oldest is the hardest! I have to set the example. Everything I've gone through will be easier for my younger sisters because my parents understand more, plus I'll be able to help them also.

Being a parent must be pretty hard. I've thought about it, getting married and having children. A parent can love their children so much that they want to lock them up and not let them grow up. To make a decision whether we can go out at night is difficult, not knowing all that goes on, where we might be and most of all if we are safe. Parents have already gone through the years of being teenagers so they really do know how we feel. But we're a part of them and they don't want any harm to come to us so they have to protect us. With Jesus in a family I believe there would always be a better understanding on both parts.

Michelle: I think everyone should share with parents because they can help. I think parents should share with their children, too.

Wendy: It depends on what mood they are in. If they are in a grumpy mood stay away but don't disobey them. If they are in a good mood it's a lot easier to talk about things.

ATMOSPHERE IN THE HOME WHEN MOM WORKED

Rochelle: When Mom worked we all had to pitch in more than usual. We just couldn't keep the house up to standard. She tried her hardest to keep everything the same.

Michelle: We never had time to see anyone. The house was a mess.

Wendy: The house wasn't as clean as when she didn't work and we couldn't have relatives come over because they would want to talk to Mom.

Jackie: I didn't like it. Everything was "yucky." The house was messy. No one could help me get to school, I had to run when I was late. We had more fights.

ATMOSPHERE IN THE HOME WHEN MOM IS NOT WORKING

Rochelle: I'm glad she's not working anymore, and she's home when we come home from school. Then she can be here to tell us not to eat so much, or to clean our rooms. Too many kids have nothing to do and nobody at home so they go other places to enjoy themselves in many ways and they're not always the right ways.

Michelle: Now everything is picked up and the house is clean. We can go places and visit people.

Wendy: The house is cleaner and we have company more often. Now the fights are stopped right away.

Jackie: I like it. The house is clean and Mom has time to help me when I need it. And now we can go places.

CHORES

Rochelle: There has always been chores to do around our house. It can get pretty messy with four girls and all of their clothes and toys. We've always been taught to clean up our messes. Doing chores is as much a part of growing up as learning how to do them. Sometimes there are fights when someone wants to get out of chores. So I usually do them myself, probably because I'm having company of some sort. My sisters will eventually learn as they get older.

Wendy: They work out good because we always have it planned. But when we clean the whole house we each pick a room, clean it and our own rooms.

Jackie: I don't like chores but have to do them so I hurry to get them over. I like the house better when we're through.

FAMILY RECREATION

Rochelle: Our family often gets together for some activity besides cleaning the house. Sometimes if I'm not busy I'll join in for a family swim. With our big family and so many relatives it's fun to get together and have picnics. As I grow older I don't attend as many family events as I have in the past. Parents have to understand that their children will grow away from these things, not forever, but just until they've fully grown up and maybe graduated from school. All in all, I think every family should try to do something together at least once a week, even if it's to go to church together on Sunday.

Wendy: You should play games together and do other things because it makes your family happier and brings it together.

Jackie: Because we've always done things as a family I don't think I'd like it if we didn't have it.

DOING MY OWN THING

Many families have prodigal sons, daughters, fathers or mothers. We have all sinned and fallen short of the glory of God. Each person in his own time, and in his own way, comes to a realization that sin and rebellion do not bring happiness or peace.

Anytime I stand before a group of persons to minister the Gospel, it is always interesting to look at the faces before me. Some are aglow with the Spirit and the joy of the Lord having already experienced salvation and the fullness of the Spirit in their lives; other faces are perplexed and puzzled as they try to figure out what is taking place at this meeting they've been invited to. Still other faces have a hunger on them—seeking, desiring to experience and to know in their own lives that truth and those blessings that have been experienced by those around them. Some faces look bored and frustrated, like they are checking out the nearest exit in hopes of making a quick escape before the meeting gets any more emotional. Yet, other faces look as if they are evaluating and scrutinizing all that is being said and done.

One evening while speaking at a Charismatic prayer meeting, among the faces I saw one that seemed to be intently measuring and taking in every word that I shared. I knew that God was doing something special for this particular person. I could hardly wait until the close of the meeting to inquire of this individual and to learn more about the life behind the face of this young man. At the conclusion of the meeting, a young lady came to me and introduced herself as Carlene. She said, "Mike, I would like you to meet my friend Dan McNew. Dan has just recently started to come to the prayer meetings and I thought you could be of some encouragement to him."

With that introduction, a young man who eagerly sat throughout the meeting measuring every word soon became a very special brother of mine in the Lord. As I inquired about Dan's past experience, again I saw before me another miracle of the new birth and a life being changed by the power of the Holy Spirit.

* * * * *

It was a cool morning in late August of 1970, as my family and I were driving from Pittsburgh, Pennsylvania, to St. Louis, Missouri. I was eighteen and going away to school. Looking back on that ride to St. Louis I don't know if I was more scared or excited about spending the next four years 600 miles from home. It sounded good telling myself that I'd be on my own, able to come and go as I pleased, to do everything I had wanted and not have someone asking me why or where I was going, or telling me I couldn't do it. At the same time though I could sense a desire to stay in the comfortable surroundings of Pittsburgh. I knew a number of people and they knew me, life was easy. But, I was leaving all that now to go to college to find out what I was going to do the rest of my life.

During my first year at school everything was going right. I was in pre-med and my grades were good, better than a "B" average. I had picked Washington University in order to play varsity football. After the second game I was in the starting backfield and making all the trips to the "away" games. I lettered that year and was looking forward to another good year.

My sophomore year went pretty much the same as my first year. One thing that was disappointing was that my grades had dropped. I knew I was partying too much but kept telling myself I would study more next year, but I never did. There were always so many other things to do.

Other things consisted of drinking, hustling women, and always searching for something more exciting to do. I began drinking more beer and experimenting with drugs. I would get high each night and then sit around and talk or listen to music. This relieved the guilt of not studying and also passed the time.

As I look back on those two years at school, I can see I was trying to fill a void inside of me with a lot of external activities. Always the void came back. Gene Neil in his book *I'm Gonna Bury You,* describes it as a God-shaped hole which only the Lord can fill. It is a realization that there is something which makes all of life worthwhile.

The next three years of my life were spent trying to fill this void, this emptiness which wouldn't leave. The things that had filled it before didn't any more.

Whenever I was depressed or listless I could always drink a few beers, call up a girl, and after two or three hours I again felt fine for a few days. It got to the point that this didn't work. So I began partying harder. Many a morning I would wake up and wonder where I had been, or how I got home. It's a scary feeling.

At one point I made up my mind that I needed "religion," and that that was going to fill this void. The incident leading to this decision was probably the most frightening experience I ever had. I was at a friend's house and we were having a barbecue. It was about 9:30 at night and we had been drinking for two hours. There was a knock on the door so I answered it. Two guys with guns were there. They were looking for drugs. They tied us up, pistol-whipped us and threatened to kill us. For some reason they changed their minds and left. It was such a relief.

The next day I woke up and thanked God for keeping me safe and made up my mind to buy a Bible and go to church. I did.

I got a Bible and began reading it but it didn't make sense. Going to church was also a letdown. It was a good feeling being there, but these same people were worrying about the same things I did. I thought that if these people who went to church every Sunday were no better off than I, what good is God anyway? Where was this peace and joy that the Bible tells about? I believed in God but He was up in the sky, not down where I was. I'd make it on my own.

I reasoned: What was I dissatisfied with? Was it my job? Was it St. Louis, was it my life style? I settled for the first two. I decided to go back home to Pittsburgh and go to school there.

I enrolled at the University of Pittsburgh and thought everything was going to be fine. That void came back, this time worse than ever. I was miserable. I didn't want to talk to anyone, I felt alone. I was fighting with my parents, struggling to get through the day, and always bored. The only time I wasn't bored was when I was praying. I would party until four or five in the morning.

Then one night in September of 1975 the phone rang. It was a wrong number, or was it? The voice sounded familiar. It was Carlene. She was calling someone else and dialed my number by mistake. Now Carlene had a habit of calling or writing just when I needed someone to talk with. As we talked, she mentioned that I seemed depressed and would I like to talk about it? I agreed to meet her.

At first I didn't have too much to say, but then a lot

of my frustrations started coming out. I told her about the drinking and the women, and how I felt there was a wall around me keeping me from reaching out to people. And how I felt I had been hurt and used by people, and I didn't want them near me. The truth was I didn't want people to get to know me. I knew what I was like and I didn't like it. If other people found out about me—what would they think?

Her response to all of this really shocked me. She said that Jesus knew what I was like and that He loved me. She shared about her life and how Jesus had changed it, and how it could be the same for me. This was the last thing I wanted to hear. I had been that route. No, religion wasn't for me. She went on telling me that if I invited Jesus into my life He would take over and fill the void. He would forgive my sins and I would start all over. Now this I wanted to hear. I could start over, a clean slate. It sounded so easy: just invite Him into your life, He would come. That's all!

That night I didn't ask Jesus to come into my life but I did promise to go to a prayer meeting. On the way home I thought about what Carlene had said. It sounded good, but . . . . . always those "but's." I had always thought religion was for old people or little children. It was comforting to the dying and good bedtime stories for children.

I promised to go with Carlene to another prayer meeting. These people were different. They talked to me and tried to make me feel at home, and didn't talk about how bad people were or how good they were. I didn't feel I needed Jesus, just some time to get my head straight and then things would be better.

The guest speaker that night, Rev. Peter Edwards from Arizona, spoke about Jesus and his relationship to Him. He talked about how Jesus had come into his life and changed it and how He answered his prayers. He was telling how exciting his life was.

Excitement, that struck a responsive chord, that's what I was looking for. After he spoke he had an altar call. I wanted this exciting life but I wasn't going to get up in front of all those people. My pride wouldn't let me move. Then all of a sudden I found myself kneeling in front of everyone praying the sinner's prayer.

The next week at the prayer meeting I was baptized in the Spirit. I was on cloud nine. I felt so good. It was a better "high" than I ever had with alcohol or anything else. A feeling like that is too good to describe with words.

The Lord has made many changes in my life. That restless feeling is gone and the peace of the Lord is in me. No longer do I spend long hours at the bar trying to find peace.

An additional blessing from the Lord is that my relationship with my parents is greatly improved. Part of the reason is because I don't come in at 4 a.m. The Lord is showing us how a Christian family should live. It has amazed me how much effect prayer can have. No longer do I wake up and wonder how I'll make it through the day. The Lord is making each day an exciting adventure.

FULLNESS AND FREEDOM

What is the role and place of the single adult in the home, church and community?

Being single has many advantages for the Kingdom of God's sake, and at the same time presents some particular problems. Some people get married just to get married. That is, they marry perhaps out of the will of God, or marry the wrong person and live a life of unpleasantness.

I have often said that I would rather be single and lonely at times than unhappily married. I believe that there is nothing on this side of heaven that brings greater joy and fulfillment of life than to be married to the right person.

As I travel across the country, I meet many single adults who are waiting for the Lord to bring that right person into their lives. Some of them may be single for just a matter of a few years, and maybe others five or ten years, and perhaps others, all of their lives. Until the time that Jesus brings the right person into their lives, how can the single adult person's life be one of joy and freedom, without the anxiety and the fear of wondering or worrying whether they are going to get married, and if so, when and to whom? Rather than fretting about all of these questions, how can their life best be lived in service to the Lord, family and community?

In past centuries, or even in more recent decades, we see that the history of church is replete with single men and women who have made a definite mark upon the church, culture, society, and country in which they lived.

Among the more recent single women who have ministered extensively throughout the body of the church are Corrie Ten Boom and Ann Kiemel. Both of these women, one quite young, and the other a gracious "senior citizen," enjoy national and international ministries of service in sharing their witness and their life with Christ Jesus.

Being single myself, and knowing what it is to experience the joy of serving the Lord, and at the same time, knowing the frustrations of coping and dealing with my own sexuality and times of loneliness, I have found great joy in encouraging other single adults to live their life for Christ, and at the same time for them to believe that God will bring to pass, in His good timing, the perfect mate in their lives. Or, if He should direct and will that they should be single for the Kingdom's sake for the rest of their lives, He will provide the grace and fulfillment for them.

In 1971 I had the opportunity of meeting Anita Guyo at a number of the local charismatic Bible studies and fellowships in the Pittsburgh area. Anita was new in the charismatic renewal as I was, and she began to discover many exciting biblical clues and promises coming to pass in her life. We had the opportunity at many of these fellowships to share our experiences and become friends. Anita is an executive secretary to the Director of Research at Calgon Consumer Products Company in Pittsburgh.

More than her career as a secretary, Anita enjoys writing for the Body Builder, a local publication for the Pittsburgh area.

I have asked Anita to share her experiences, place, insights, and reflections on her role as a single adult.

* * * * *

Our present-day society has programmed most women to rate their success and value in life by the marital status. The single girl is constantly confronted with the much-overworked questions of why she isn't married yet or when is she planning to get married. The pressure soon makes many girls vulnerable to the torment of Satan. He quickly uses the opportunity to bring many girls into a fretful state of restlessness, and to some extent self-condemnation over their popularity status.

The world is selling a style of living that is completely opposed to God's Word. The system uses the terms freedom, self-expression, and "do your own thing" quite precariously. Love has become a household expression synonymous with lust, selfishness and "no commitment."

This "liberation" philosophy has produced more divorces, frightening increases in suicide, a phenomenal number of abortions and alienated children with blown minds and much insecurity. Homes are disintegrating, unhappiness and boredom set the mood, and obsessions with sex and materialism hold people in tight bondages. "Living together," prostitution and gambling are freely endorsed as people grope in every possible direction to find peace, love, satisfaction and fulfillment in their lives. Yet, most scoff at the simple message of God's Word which tells us the fullness of life is found in Jesus Christ.

The quality of life Jesus offers is far above the meager, bargain-basement life style the world offers so cheaply. Life in Jesus speaks of peace, joy, stability, security and victory beginning right now and throughout the future.

The peace of Jesus brings quietness into our inner selves. It sets us free from struggling and anxieties. Through it we can know who we are, to whom we belong, and where we are going. This peace is not dependent upon circumstances.

His peace resides in us because of His very presence within us.

One of the best witnesses to many of my single female Christian and non-Christian friends is the joy, peace and stability evidenced in my life as a single person. Sometimes it is hard to find an appropriate expression to successfully convince others who are searching for self-satisfaction and a meaningful life that it will only be born when they meet Jesus and enter into a personal relationship with the Father through Him.

It is not essential that one find the right job, marry the "perfect" man, or succeed in finding acceptance by his or her peers. The abundant life becomes our possession when we discover what the heart of God is really like. He accepts us completely and we are wanted. The greatest word that Jesus revealed to us was "Father."

The will of the Father for us to live an abundant life—to be fulfilled, to be able in the most uncomplicated way, to translate that overcoming power of Jesus into our own personal lives as single Christians can only come when we trust Him enough to give Him control over our lives.

Reflecting on the past five years since I accepted Jesus as my Lord and Saviour and received the baptism of the Holy Spirit, I can recall many wonderful moments and times of fellowship with the Lord. Reluctantly, though, I also have to admit times of failing Him, incidents of falling into temptations, and periods of slipping away from His peace and love. These were times when I failed to rest my entire being on the Greater One within me—when I looked to my own ability and withdrew my availability to Christ within.

We may be tempted to think that Jesus isn't all one needs. We slip back into self-centeredness and begin to look to *our capability* to attain our wants and desires. We take our eyes off the Resident Power within and begin to look in other directions for satisfaction, forgetting that it is only Jesus who can fill any vacuums in our lives. The world's attractions continually seek to win our attention from the One who holds it all together. One soon discovers, usually after much useless struggling, that what the world offers is very plastic, shallow and temporal. We soon experience disenchantment when we realize that the "things" we were so convinced we had to have never satisfy permanently. Only the Lord can offer complete satisfaction. True fulfillment must first be established in the spirit of a person and is never found by physical or material acquisitions.

Much of the struggling to gain "liberation" and to overcome "put down" feelings ceases when one accepts Jesus as Lord and Saviour. Through Him we can be emancipated from the pressures bombarding us concerning the importance of career fulfillment and "fitting" in with just the right people. If we give Him our all He quickly gives us His all in exchange and we begin to fit into His perfect plans. Thus, the fear of rejection, boredom, and the threatening opinions of others lose their hold on us and we begin to experience the reality of divine liberation.

Many individuals place a false sense of reality on marriage, elevating it to a position where it has become a sort of magic formula or cure-all for happiness and contentment. Many want to pin marriage on like a "happy button" and instantly solve all their problems of loneliness, insecurity and lack of purpose in life.

True liberating security is found only in Christ. If we award Him second place in our lives, single or married, the end result will always be a lack of satisfaction and frustration in trying to uncover the missing element to our peace, joy and true purpose for living.

Many Christians experience a dilemma over the dating problem, especially when it comes to dating unbelievers. God's Word states that light has no fellowship with darkness. Any prolonged relationship with a person not totally committed to Jesus Christ will ultimately impede the

Christian walk.

Our society takes a very lenient view on moral conduct and suggest a "free style" of living, giving persons the chance to set their own standards. Unfortunately this morally bankrupt system rather than producing "free spirits," is resulting in many becoming entrapped in a prison of self, with problems of guilt, frustration and spiritual and emotional barrenness. God's laws restricting any sexual activity to the protection of the marriage bond is just one more principle of His ever-perfect plan for our greatest well-being. He chose to protect us against future emotional psychological and physical scars which would leave a very detrimental effect on our total well-being.

Others opinions of your life style may be critical, but the only opinion we need be concerned with is God's opinion of us. You may not be an "average" person, but you are normal, taking such a stand, for Christianity is the only true normal way of life!

Adding to the single girl's dismay are the constant opinions and pressures from friends and family. She often finds herself the object of their conniving and maneuvering to bring together what they consider the "perfect couple," thereby forgetting the Scripture "What God hath brought together." If we look into God's Word we find that He is the one who brought Eve to Adam. There was no attempt on Adam's part to go and find her. The Lord brought Eve to his side. By Adam's example one can learn that as we delight in the Lord and seek His will first the wants and desires of the heart will be granted. Many young people seem to face a certain difficulty in releasing this part of their will to the Lord. Seemingly, it proves to be the one personal desire they find hardest to submit to God's goodness and perfect wisdom. Many are beset with doubt that their Heavenly Father could perform a better job in choosing their life partner than they themselves could do. Henceforth, unnecessary burdens are experienced which rob them of joy and freedom in the Spirit.

Many girls tend to experience guilt because in reality they are actually harboring fear in permitting the Lord total freedom to operate in this very special and sensitive desire of their hearts. Many rebel at the idea of accepting God's total lordship in choosing a husband for them. Others continue in a spirit of rebellion because they are lending the enemy some attention by listening to his nagging lies, such as, "You're going to end up with someone you don't really like; The Lord isn't going to bring someone to you because you would then place Jesus second in your life; You already have had your chance, but you missed it."

With others the marriage problem has become idolatrous. The desire for marriage has become an idol of worship and has replaced the desire for communion and fellowship with the Lord, pushing Him into a second-rate position.

Guilt can also occur when one has the desire for marriage, but through erroneous teaching has been persuaded that Paul is against the union. It would be a contradiction for Paul to call something bad which God had ordained and intended for His glory. The teaching of Paul for some to postpone marriage or remain single was directed to a community of people in a particular period of time when, because of tremendous persecution, it would have been advantageous for them not to take on any added responsibilities. His later discourse on the type of love that a marriage should reflect reveals that he held the marriage unit as something very sacred, and certainly blessed of God.

The most important question one should submit to the Father is: "What is your will for me concerning marriage; in which state can I serve You the most effectively?" Many single women, such as Corrie Ten Boom or Roxanne Brant, live life to the fullest as they devote their entire time, talent and personality to the Lord's service.

It is in yielding to Jesus daily as He lovingly and graciously unfolds His perfect plans for our lives that we can begin to know true freedom and fullness of life. Single or married, our maximum achievements and greatest experiences of joy will be those moments when we have confidently trusted Jesus and have done our best to walk in His will.

If you are the Christian in the household, much of the mood set is going to depend upon your attitude. You have to assume the responsibility to be flexible—to fit in with alterations that may not be all that agreeable to your personal desires. But, in your chosen position as God's channel of blessing you are called to be a peacemaker—to walk the extra mile. Perhaps some of the greatest moments in our lives are those times when we act in a spirit of love.

Single or married, our maximum achievements and greatest experiences of joy will be those times when we know we have done His will.

Food For Thought For Singles:
1. Learning to love one's self is crucial to loving others.
2. Make good use of any free time to mature in your knowledge of the Master.
3. Learn how to go to God yourself for all your needs.
4. Invest part of your time in Christian service.
5. Replace self-centeredness with a keen sensitivity to needs of others.
6. Learn to accept responsibilities and become more disciplined in performing any task delegated to you.
7. Your ability and performance of your job should be done to the Lord's glory.
8. All Christians are called upon to be hospitable.
9. Explore new fields of employment for which you could qualify, or begin to prepare yourself.
10. Be more adventurous. Consider new sports or new

places to go.

11. Look for ways to become more creative (art, crafts, music, etc.).

GROWING IN LOVE

As the plane took off from San Diego to Monterey, I fastened my seat belt and prayed a paraphrased version of the Twenty-third Psalm by my friend Bill Paris:

The Lord is my Pilot, my plane is well equipped. He maketh me to fly in clear skies. He guideth me through the still air.

He keepeth my engine running; He guideth me across the country for his name's sake.

Yea, though I fly through the thunderstorms, I am not afraid for my Pilot is with me. His companionship stablilzes me.

He prepares an airstrip in the midst of IFR (bad weather conditions). He setteth up my approach. My fuel tank overfloweth.

Surely safety and mercy shall be with me all the days of my life, and I shall dwell in my Lord's hangar forever.

As I concluded the prayer, the plane was well in the air and I began to greatly anticipate my visit with Dr. Bob Cuva and his wife Mary.

I also began to think about my desire to invite them to share in this book. Many thoughts streamed through my mind and I tried to decide what would be the most appropriate subject for their sharing. First I thought about the mother and daughter relationships; the Cuva's have five daughters and Mary has a beautiful relationship with each of them. But then I finally concluded that Bob should write this chapter.

As I stepped off the plane there was Bob with his big smile, open arms, and loving heart to give me his usual warm greeting.

"Where is Mary?" I asked.

"Well, Mike, she and the girls are back home whipping up a delicious gourmet dinner for you," he replied.

One day Bob, the dentist, said, "Mike, while you are here and I am available for these few days, I would like to check your teeth and do any necessary dental work for you."

The next day Bob took me to his very beautiful office, and as I sat in the dental chair, he tilted it back and I glanced to the ceiling and saw, "Smile, Jesus Loves You," and "Those Who Wait Upon the Lord Shall Renew Their Strength." There, tacked all over the ceiling, were many colorful Jesus posters, signs and banners.

I not only had my teeth cleaned, checked and filled, but my heart was blessed as I read the various posters and saw Dr. Bob's big bright face aglow with the love of Jesus looking down and injecting the novocaine with his special Christian T.L.C.

After Bob had completed my dental work, we talked a bit about the necessity and benefits of not only scrubbing teeth regularly, but using dental floss, and taking other precautions in maintaining good dental hygiene. I shared with

Bob how inconvenient it is for me to dental floss my teeth on a regular basis because of being so busy and on the go much of the time, but that I would make a special effort to be more faithful in this regard. I said to him, "Bob, I am not going to just dental floss my teeth, but I am going to turn it into a time of praise and thank the Lord for you and the family for the joy you have been to me, and also that the Holy Spirit will continue to use you to introduce many of your patients to our living Saviour."

* * * * *

For the first nine years of our marriage, Mary and I discovered our union was not growing. We each had found separate interests in life, and we were simply tolerating one another. I would plunge into my work, and then pursue the distractions of golf, hunting and weekend sports. Mary would involve herself with social clubs, gourmet cooking, and elegant home parties. In spite of all of our activity, we had become strangers to one another in our own home. We found it awkward to accept or encourage one another through the many problems that are common to every family.

Eventually, as friction increased, we would try to change the other to conveniently fit into our personal desires and ambitions. Our quarrels to get our own way would also bring feelings of loneliness and depression. Our children were forced into the captivity of television, as we gave them less and less of ourselves. The children never wanted for things, but they were truly neglected.

Through the friction in our marriage, I became aware of my need for religion. I began attending a daily early-morning Mass, and found myself, for the first time, talking to Jesus. In a few weeks I noticed a change coming over me. I had a new inner peace which I had never experienced before.

Although I could not express it yet, I knew I had met the Lord. (This was in the early part of 1972.)

I was invited to attend a Cursillo weekend. A group of men from that Cursillo weekend began to meet weekly for Bible reading and prayer. After several months most of us had experienced a deeper relationship with Jesus and also the baptism of the Holy Spirit. Mary received the baptism of the Holy Spirit four months after myself.

After our experience, we both yearned for spiritual food from the Holy Scriptures. We found ourselves visiting other churches, listening to inspired teachers, and beginning to feed on the truth in God's Word. We became active in the weekly prayer meetings. The Lord called me to be the leader of the prayer group, with Mary supporting me through her love and encouragement.

Prayer has brought a new dimension into our lives. Both Mary and I pray earnestly for our relatives and friends, those who know Christ, and those who do not. On two occasions the Lord revealed to us during our time of prayer, that it was His will for us to spend our annual vacation with Mary's parents in Nebraska. Both vacations proved to be a time of family ministry, seeing souls saved, and Mary's parents come into a personal relationship with Jesus.

We have witnessed healings in our own family as a direct answer to prayer. One day our daughter Christina had her fingers smashed in the car door. By the power of prayer Jesus straightened her fingers and immediately took away the pain. Through prayer the Lord has revealed to us where to find things that have been lost, healed fevers, stopped hiccups, headaches, and cured my chronic stomach problem.

Besides a new relationship with Himself, the Lord began a new relationship between ourselves and our children.

God has shown us as parents that we do not possess our children, but rather, they belong to Him, and we are merely stewards of His possessions. We have had to learn to allow them to be themselves, and to make decisions on their own. While we cannot always allow them the way of their decision, we realize it is important for them to express their desire. One way in which we allow this is for the children to choose what they would like to do on Sunday, which is our family day. We also have what we call "town house meetings." These are times when our children can express themselves concerning changes they would like within the home, or a time to discuss problems among themselves.

As Christian parents we found it not only important to give our children guidance in the freedom of choice, but also to give them instruction in the truths of God. Some of these principles are such as forgiving one another (Matthew 18:21-25); or explaining the truth that "what you sow is what you reap" (Galatians 6:7); or the generous spirit behind liberal giving (Proverbs 11:24). When one of our children offends someone, we instruct them to go to the person and tell them they are sorry. Our children are learning that when they show kindness they will reap kindness; when they sow jealousy, they reap jealousy.

Our marriage began to heal soon after Jesus came into our lives. In that beginning experience His presence was felt through our whole being. Then, after a year or so, we no longer felt His presence as we had earlier. In the beginning it was easy to love each other because we felt loving. Then as the loving feeling decreased, so did our relationship with one another. Through this, God taught us that to love the way He loves, requires an act of our will and not the dependence upon a "lovely feeling."

An area of our relationship in which we are growing today, is that in the acceptance of one another. We came to realize that since God accepts us just the way we are, then we are to accept each other the same way. An example of this can be illustrated in what was my judgmental concern for Mary's "spirituality." I would criticize her for failing to read the Bible or pray as much as I thought she should. This in turn drove a wedge between our relationship. Jesus showed me that I was not accepting her just as she was. As I began to accept her, I then began to see wonderful changes begin to occur in her life. At the same time, the Lord began to deal with Mary concerning her attitudes about the freedom of my life.

Recently the Lord has given us a new depth of love for each other. We are truly caring for each other and desiring the other to be happy in what they are doing. Only the Lord Jesus can produce this kind of love—which had been absent for so long in our marriage.

HOW OLD IS TOO OLD?

Dad recently retired from the Westinghouse as a welder. My brother Richard, his family, and I hosted a retirement party for him, and because it was a surprise, Dad was deeply touched. It was also during this time that the Holy Spirit began doing a beautiful work in his life and he began changing in many ways.

My father, like most men, did not want to go from a complete full working schedule to simply doing nothing. Even though he loved and enjoyed golf, bowling, reading the newspaper and novels, and watching television, he still needed something to fill in many of the hours of the day or evening.

Dad spent the early days of his retirement building a recreation room in the basement of my brother's home, and building a den, library and office for me in his own home.

In all the years that I was in college and seminary away from home, and the years that I spent on the road traveling, I never received any letters from my father. He always delegated the job of letter writing to my mother. As the Lord began to deal with me, He impressed me to address my letters home "Dear Dad and Mom," rather than "Dear Mom and Dad." The Lord was showing me in various significant ways how fathers are to be the head of the home.

All the years that my father worked at the Westinghouse, he worked second shift, four to twelve, and was never home in the evenings when my brother and I came home from school. Because of this I never saw much of my father, nor was I very close to him. However, during the time he was building my office, the Lord was drawing us much closer together. As I began addressing my letters to "Dear Dad and Mom," I found my father began writing back to me. Not only were his letters well written, but they were a joy to read. They were short and to the point, but loaded with meaning and love. Among the favorite letters I received from him was the following: "Dear Michael, I am busily at work building your den, library and office. I am running into many difficulties in construction and design. The Lord is helping me all along the way. I can assure you Michael, that I am dipping down into the 'bottom of the barrel' of my hidden talent and skills to make this job for you second-to-none. With much love, Dad."

Wow . . . what a letter! Not only was it a confirmation that the work was being done on the den with my being in California and my parents home in Pennsylvania, but more than that it was a confirmation of my dad's genuine love for me. As he found it difficult to express his love in words, more often then not, he showed it in what he "did" rather than what he "said."

Six months later when I arrived home for Christmas, the job was completed! All our relatives and friends who came to our home agreed that he had done a magnificent job. I enjoy this den for the time and the place that it affords me to study, prepare for ministering, entertain and write. More than that, every part of that den is an expression of my dad's tender loving care.

Dad had a habit of using the Lord's name quite lightly in speech at times. The whole time he was building my den, *my mom told me that he never once used the Lord's name in vain or cussed as he was working. If things went wrong, he would simply say, "Praise the Lord" and trust in Jesus to help him every step of the way.*

Shortly after my father retired, I invited him to come to one of the meetings where I was sharing and preaching at St. Martin's Church. When I was introduced to speak, I began to share the message by speaking of some things about my family, and I asked Dad to come forward and introduced him to all the people present there that evening. After I made this introduction, I asked all the "senior citizens" to stand and for those around them to lay their hands upon them that we might agree in prayer together. We asked the Lord to abundantly bless my father and all our parents and grandparents that their latter years would be filled with joy, peace and strength in Christ.

When people grow old or mature in years they have one of two options before them. First, they can become old, cranky, miserable and unpleasant to live with; or secondly, they can be those "senior citizens" that young people will look up to and admire because of the peace, love and joy that is evidenced in their lives.

I have personally witnessed a ministry that has a tremendous outreach to those living in their "golden years." Fred and Dorothy Brown extended a warm welcome to me at the Prayer House in Tucson, Arizona, where I went to share the Good News for a few days.

In this chapter, Fred and Dorothy answer for us, HOW TO BE RETIRED, BUT NOT SO TIRED. Fred recently retired from management at Homestead Steel in Pennsylvania, and Dorothy retired as assistant editor and columnist for the TIMES EXPRESS in Monroeville, Pennsylvania.

In their early retirement, the Lord filled in their hours and time with more activity, work and blessing than they ever experienced in their former jobs. The following is an account of how these two young retirees have been a blessing to senior citizens and are helping them not to just simply fill their life with years, but to fill their years with abundant life in Jesus.

* * * * *

It all began in 1971 when the Lord called us out of our jobs and we found ourselves retired at the early ages of 45 and 48. As that retirement went into effect we learned the difference between the Lord's PERMISSIVE will and his PERFECT will. We asked Jesus for a year to travel before going into full-time service. We thought we had to have that year to be together and see the country. After six months we were bored!

We were in Montreal, and while we loved it as a city and witnessed much about the baptism of the Holy Spirit we were unfulfilled, restless and ill. Dottie contracted a lung condition that the strongest antibiotics would not cure. It was either return to Pittsburgh for extensive x-rays, or seek a warm, dry climate. As we chose to do the latter we realized the Lord could be allowing the affliction to lead us to that desert in which we said WE would never live!

We prayed that if this were indeed true, Jesus would heal Dottie, but even if He did not, we would go to the desert. The next day all pain was gone from her chest! And we had made a deal with the Lord. So we headed for Tucson.

As directors of The Prayer House in Tucson, we have seen Jesus transform lives from five to 95. Tucson is basically a retirement town and when we first came to The Prayer House our ministry was mostly to retired persons. It's changed to include a large and beautiful family in Christ, of all ages, with no meddling or complaining members.

How is this possible? How can 50 persons watch a teaching tape with sharing, singing and fellowship when the ages represented 80, 60, 40, 20 and five, and everywhere in between? Jesus makes the difference! He's the bridge across the troubled waters of the generation gap.

Retired persons can fall into three categories: those who know all *about* Jesus but do not *know* Jesus; those who know Jesus but do not walk and talk with Him; and those who are rejoicing and walking in His Holy Spirit.

Being the resident director of a Prayer House can be an exciting ministry for any retired but not-so-tired person. Anyone who has a home can turn it into a Prayer House if willing to give up ownership, give it to the Lord; become incorporated as a non-profit organization; and let Jesus support it and use it. He will! And there is such a need. Many churches today do not offer the warm, personal fellowship to be found at a non-denominational, Spirit-filled house that belongs, along with everything in it, to Jesus. Lawyer's fees for incorporation may take someone's "nest egg" but what better way could it be put to use? Who needs a "nest egg" when we have God's promises concerning ALL little birds!

The primary reason of being for any Prayer House is, of course, prayer. There are endless telephone requests, many hours spent in intercessory prayer, and sleepless nights spent with those in dire need who have knocked on the door, which is always open 24 hours a day at the chapel at Prayer House in Tucson.

Then there is counseling of married couples, teen-agers, widows, divorced persons, etc., in addition to Bible studies, prayer meetings and fellowship gatherings.

A Prayer House ministry can be physically exhausting and emotionally draining, but only to the extent that the directors allow it to be. Much prayer in connection with any step of faith such as this is necessary, however. While it may be the perfect way to serve for some, it could be too spiritually taxing for others.

The Prayer House has been a blessing in our lives, but

the best part of all is "growing" together with the other members of the Body in the ministry. God the Father has answered impossible prayers, Jesus has saved and baptized hundreds, and the power of the Holy Spirit has healed bodies and memories. There have been teaching sessions, mini-conferences, and most wonderful experiences in worship through music.

The schedule is full to bursting. A youth group, high school and college age, has just been added. We will send a sample calendar to anyone interested in what goes on in a Prayer House ministry (but do not advise as heavy a schedule). Address requests to: The Prayer House, 2449 E. 7th St., Tucson, AZ 85719.

The Prayer House is truly a House of the Lord, a working miracle itself, and only He has made it so. And He provides for it through those who love it.

There are also other ministries for retired persons: book ministries; Vista and Peace Corps projects that offer a way into countries where missionaries cannot go; prison visitation ministries; working in the halfway houses, and many other ways of serving that can be found through prayer, in asking God's direction and will for retirement years.

We have only tried to say: "Fear not, Jesus is in love with retired persons! To Him there are no maidens too old to fill their lamps; no laborers too late to work in the fields!"

I BELIEVE

When the Lord healed my eyes after wearing glasses for 30 years, I found great joy in sharing my blessing with others. What was even more remarkable than the healing of my eyes, was that whenever I shared my testimony, I found the Lord did for others what He has done for me.

Healing takes place in various ways. Jesus ministers differently according to each individual need as we read the Gospel narrative. Some persons receive healing as the Word of God is being preached. Their faith just simply responds to the proclamation of the Gospel and they are healed. Others are strengthened as they are anointed with oil. Still others are healed as they receive prayer and the laying on of hands. Sometimes it is enough to simply come before God in the privacy of one's own home and in prayer ask Jesus for His healing touch. People have been healed in the context of a service at an evangelistic crusade or at a prayer meeting. Many have experienced healing after the reception of the Eucharist or the Sacrament of Healing.

I believe that a physical healing not only affects our personal lives and the lives of our family, but also the life of our community. Our believing friends rejoice and give thanks and praise for the great and wonderful things that our risen Lord has done and is doing among His people today.

Unbelieving relatives or friends sit up and take notice and their faith is challenged when we are healed. That is, they no longer can sit back and think in terms of just the mechanics or the formalism of religion; but rather they must come to terms with IS JESUS ALIVE? and ARE THESE HEALINGS REALLY FOR REAL?

I have asked Barbara DeRoche to share with you her own response to the Lord's healing grace, and the effect it has had upon her and her family.

* * * * *

I believe:

God's Word is as true today as it was in Bible times.

That we should pray according to God's will and His will is in His Word. " . . . and this is the confidence that we have in him, that if we ask anything according to his will, he heareth us: and if we know he heareth us, whatsoever we ask, we know that we have the petition that we desired of him" (I John 5:14-15).

We must expect God to answer our prayers, thanking and praising God for it. You will receive all that you pray for, provided you have faith (Matthew 21:21).

We must stand on the authority of the Word, act upon it and learn to incorporate it into our daily lives.

This has not been an easy task in regards to an unsaved family.

As I look back over the past three years since I have been baptized in the Holy Spirit, I can see the Lord working in our family.

Before the Holy Spirit came into our lives, our marriage was happy by the world's standards. We have three lovely daughters, a new home, and good health. Louis and I have never had any difficulties in our marriage; in fact, we are considered to have an ideal marriage by many of our friends. We attend Mass as a family every Sunday, get along better than most and often conducted activities together. What more could anyone ask?

With all that we had I began to experience a deep hunger for God.

I began attending a local Charismatic prayer meeting, and it was at one of these prayer meetings that Evangelist Michael Gaydos gave his testimony.

After Mike's testimony Mass was begun and the Eucharist was elevated after the consecration. I bowed my head and said, "My Lord and my God." I felt the healing power of the Lord spread through my entire body. At that moment I removed the glasses that I had worn for 17 years.

Glasses had become so much a part of my life that I could not be without them for more than one hour without becoming physically ill. I had 20:40 vision in one eye and 20:30 in the other; an astigmatism and an extreme sensitivity to light.

In Mike's testimony he mentioned that God would give a Christmas gift that only He could give. At that time I had no idea what lay in store. On December 11, 1973, my eyes were healed; on December 24 my husband Louis went to confession, and on Christmas day he received Holy Communion—after an absence of 17 years. Only God could have accomplished that!

Healing was an uncommon occurrence at our prayer meetings. I soon saw people pointing fingers at me saying, "She is the one who was healed. She wore thick glasses and was almost blind." The stories about me were exaggerated, and placed doubts in my mind.

Satan attacked me and tormented my life with nightmares of humiliation with accusations such as: *Stupid, how do you know you will be able to see tomorrow? You will be made a fool in the parish when you are forced to put your glasses on.* Satan continued to batter me, implanting fears into my heart until I lost my healing. I could not see. The headaches returned and upset stomachs plagued me until I again placed my glasses on. I was defeated and crushed.

In all of this turmoil God spoke to my spirit: *What is more important to you, what people will say, or that I have healed your eyes?* God was right! I was more concerned with personal pride than in receiving what God had chosen to bless me with. But I still could not see.

After three days Louis encouraged me to remove the glasses. Although he did not believe in healing, he said, "You managed without them for this long, I know you can see."

At this point my faith was very weak, but I used what little faith I had and vowed that I would never again wear my glasses because God *had* healed my eyes. "Faith is the substance of things hoped for, the evidence of things not seen" (Hebrews 11:1). My sight gradually returned over a period of days as I read the word of God, thanking and praising Him.

I then began to feel the Lord working within our family. Cherie and Lynn, two of our daughters, began to play their guitars at the prayer meetings. Often at night we would gather together for the girls to play and sing songs of praise unto the Lord. We became closer as a family, united in the love of Christ.

I felt the Lord telling me to invite Mike to come to conduct a healing service at our prayer meeting at Chalmette. Mike invited the people to receive the baptism of the Holy Spirit. Louis was so impressed with Mike's love for people and his service that he stood to receive the Holy Spirit. He had never been able to fully surrender to the Lord before this and receive all that the Lord had for him.

I'M LEARNING

One day Mark Goodman and I were enjoying a ride up the chairlift at Seven Springs for some skiing. As we were sharing our favorite Scripture passages, I asked him how much time he spent each day in the word. Mark responded by saying he spent a half hour in study, and a half hour in meditation in the morning, and the same at night.

We continued to talking about some of the special blessings and joys, as well as some of the problems of living at home under the headship of parents, and about such responsibilities as paying rent, freedom to come and go, et cetera.

It would have been impossible for me to have traveled as much as I have were it not for good parents who took care of my mail and other details of the ministry. For me it has been a great joy to stay at home as a single adult. At the same time it has been a burden for at times my dad and mom didn't fully understand my commitment and feel the burden of my heart for the ministry, nor did they fully understand what it was to walk with the Lord in a deep personal way and be led by His Holy Spirit. There have been times that I would be going through valley experiences and my parents thought there was something wrong. But I couldn't fully communicate some of these experiences to them. So, along with the special joys, were special problems.

Mark is a single male adult who lives at home, goes to college and works as an insurance salesman. I have asked him to share something of his life as a single adult in regard to his relationship to the Lord, the Word, and his responsibility to his parents since he is living under the same roof.

* * * * *

In 1965, at the age of 12, I became a member of the family of God. Unfortunately, this had no great effect on my life until 1972. At that time I began realizing how foolish I had been through my disobedience to God by not giving Him my whole life (as He so unselfishly gave His for me).

I began to study God's Word, and to my astonishment my first lesson was in obedience, not to God but to my parents. It wasn't that I was always in trouble or openly rebellious, but I did do many things behind their backs that I knew were contrary to their wishes.

It became obvious to me that I had to change, and I did for we are told in Colossians 3:20 (NAS): "Children obey your parents in everything for this is well-pleasing to the Lord." Obedience did not come automatically, it is still a conscious decision, along with lots of help from the Lord and earnest effort on my part.

I discovered that God *commands* us to obey our parents, and does not give us the option to obey or not to obey. Exodus 20:12 reads: "Honor thy father and thy mother, that thy days may be long upon the land which the Lord thy God giveth thee." And also, "Children obey your parents in the Lord: for this is right. Honor thy father and mother; which is the first commandment with a promise that it may be well with thee, and thou mayest live long on the earth" (Ephesians 6:1-3).

Obedience was not easy for me, but when I am reminded that my relationship with God depends on my relationship with my parents and I obey them out of love, I am well on my way toward a rich, full and rewarding relationship with the Lord Jesus Christ.

Being single and living at home required that I put great emphasis on my relationship with my parents. They provide a home, food and a warm loving environment in which to grow as a Christian. Those who are married have their spouse to comfort and encourage them in time of need. Whereas my relationship must be such that my parents and I can comfort each other.

One of the areas that greatly hindered my spiritual growth was my continued relationship with old friends. There was an emptiness of not having close friends in which to confide so I went to others looking for close relationships. I did not have many Christian friends nor did I try to develop relationships with them. I thought this void could be filled by increasing my friendship with non-Christians. I discovered that by visiting and going with them to social events they assumed that my convictions were the same as theirs. My likes, beliefs and morals were being associated with those of my friends even though they knew nothing of my Jesus. It was very hard for me not to be influenced by their actions. Eventually I discovered I was not standing up for Christ at all but was giving Him a back seat. By spending most of my time in fellowship with non-Christians I began to regress to my old habits. II Corinthians 5:17 wasn't real in my life. Then one day while leafing through the Bible I read this in Psalm 1: "Blessed is the man who does not walk in the counsel of the wicked, nor stand in the path of sinners, nor sit in the seat of the scoffers!" (NAS). Needless to say, this spoke to me. And, also, I read in I Corinthians 15:33: "Be not decived: evil communications corrupt good manners." Not that we are to cut off all relationships with non-Christians, but to keep them in proper perspective: Christ comes first. Christians are to meet with non-Christians for the purpose of being an example of a disciple of Jesus.

The majority of my time needed to be spent with Christian people. I needed to cultivate relationships with other Christians in order that their witness would strengthen me and give me courage when faced with situations involving my non-Christian friends and the compromises that arose through those associations.

The single most helpful tool available to me has been God's Word. "Heaven and earth shall pass away: but my words shall not pass away" (Luke 21:33). Jesus himself comes alive through His Word. Although my parents are my closest Christian fellowship, I find times when my life seems very lonely, and during these periods God's Word means the most to me. The life found in the Scriptures gives me the comfort and strength I need.

A great deal of my early Christian life was spent asking questions and trying to understand God, but often to no avail. I could have had my questions answered had I spent more time studying the Bible. I was unaware that God would reveal to me all the answers to my questions and give me peace and joy through the study of His Word. The long periods without the Word left me weak spiritually. When one goes without eating in the physical one soon experiences weakness and fatigue. A similar weakness of the Spirit occurred in me because I did not feed on the Word and I became a target for Satan. "Man doth not live by bread alone, but by every word that proceedeth out of the mouth of the Lord . . ." (Deuteronomy 8:3).

The Lord has been instructing me regarding my expression of faith to others and how it is intertwined with studying the Word. I Peter 3:15 (NAS) tells us "Always being ready to make a defense to everyone who asks you to give an account for the hope that is in you, yet with gentleness and reverence." I cannot give a correct answer for my "defense" if I am not acquainted with the Word.

I used to wonder about God's purpose for my life. I would go to school, work, *et cetera,* but there was seemingly no clear direction in which to concentrate my efforts. I wanted to be successful in the business community, I wanted good grades in college, but what was my motive? God seemed to say to me: *Mark, you want success for yourself, for your glory and your desire of prestige and position in the community. All of this for your benefit, but not mine. In your college work you want recognition and status for your own desires. If you want my blessings, your priorities must change. I want people to recognize you for your love and commitment to me. I want people to say you are a success because of your devotion to me. Give me the praise for your success for it is I who have provided the way.*

This was a turning point in my life, to concentrate my efforts to bring glory to God. I had to surrender my ambitions to the Lord so now my only desire is to serve Him.

LETTING GO

Can you imagine celebrating a twenty-fifth wedding anniversary and still, after all those years of marriage, being able to learn, grow, explore, and mature together in Christ!

The Strobles are exactly this kind of couple. John has a bachelor of science degree in mechanical engineering, as well as two masters degrees—one in education and one in business. He has been with the Air Force for 29 years as a navigator and educator. Betty, who has a bachelor of science in nursing, was chosen "Travis Air Force Wife of the Year" in 1972, and is the mother of four children.

After all these years of study and serving in the Air Force in many states and countries throughout the world, John, Betty and their daughter are presently enrolled in a Charismatic Bible College to learn more of God's Word.

It was during a speaking engagement at the Air Force Base in Travis that I first met the Stroble family. They were very young in the Spirit at that time, and it amazed and inspired me to return to their home in subsequent years and observe their continual growth in faith.

Often people think of "saints" in terms of those who lived centuries ago, wore long flowing robes, had halos around them, spent all their waking hours in prayer, and lived very holy lives withdrawn from the world about them. The more I reflect upon the Scriptures and observe life, I have come to realize that in addition to these mystical individuals, among God's great saints, are those fathers and mothers who diligently undertake and faithfully exercise their responsibility, devotion, and care in raising those children the Lord has blessed them with. Raising a family today is no easy task. Love, joy, peace, long-suffering, gentleness, goodness, faith, meekness, and temperance are the nine fruits of the Holy Spirit and the mark of holiness that we see in parents who seriously, yet lovingly, follow Christ in raising their children according to biblical principles.

I am delighted that John and Betty, out of their vast experience traveling in the Air Force, and yet with their academic degrees, and most especially their love for Jesus, can share with us some of the growing pains they have as parents in cutting the umbilical cord and commending their children unto the Lord.

* * * * *

Because hindsight is so much broader than when one is in the actual situation, I can now think of two instances in Scripture where God shows us how to "let go." In the Old Testament God asks Abraham to offer up his beloved son, Isaac, and because of this obedience God spared Isaac, and Abraham was fit to be called "father of all nations." In the New Testament God gives us the perfect example to follow. Because He let go of His Son, Jesus, even unto an inhuman death, all of mankind was again restored in God's eyes.

Of course, I must admit neither of these two stories came to my mind when our first son decided to leave home secretly.

The first day my human self got in the way by making phone calls to our son's friends, and a trip to the college where he was last seen. Both of these brought no results as I was in half-hearted prayer because of fear.

As the days passed I found myself in constant communication with God—pleading, crying, begging Him to have Steve return home. Through those days God taught me how to put my trust in Him alone because He showed me how helpless I was without Him!

By the end of seven days God had me resting and trusting in Him because I had no earthly help from anyone. My husband was off on a seven-day trip at the time. When he did return it was a couple of hours before I could break the news to him.

On the tenth day friends in Colorado called to let us know that Steve had stopped and visited their son and that he was fine and was probably headed for Texas to visit some friends. Our first thoughts were to call the Highway Patrol in Colorado to pick Steve up and send him home—until we remembered we had given him to God.

One night at 11 p.m. I answered the phone and I heard: "Mom, I want to come home. I'm out of money. Would you please wire some to the airport in Houston?" Words cannot express my heartfelt thanks to God at that very moment! Within seven hours our son was back with us. When we had "let go" and allowed God to work in his life and in ours we were all changed for the better. It was the longest fourteen days we have lived through.

As our second son, John, went through high school, he developed a strong interest in police work and joined the police cadets which were sponsored by the local police department. In this organization teen-agers were taught to assist patrolmen and other members of the department. During the cadet phase we were happy that our son was on the right side of the law enforcement and that he was learning the evils of drug usage and other crimes. It appeared to us then that he was not involved in any dangerous situations.

All this changed when he reached the age of eighteen and joined the Police Reserves which were still a volunteer, non-paid adjunct to the Police Department. On one night patrol he helped capture armed robbers who shot at the police and one robber was killed.

As he let his hair grow to shoulder length and grew a mustache we wondered what was happening to him. He had volunteered to play the part of a drug-user to obtain positive and comprehensive evidence to break up a drug-pushing ring in town and to convict the dope-peddlers. No longer was our son playing "cops and robbers," and we as parents were mightily concerned about his survival.

Our communication with his police supervisors helped to lessen our concern for his safety, but we had the nagging feeling that they were using him to the fullest and were not concerned with arresting and convicting the drug-pushers, and concluded that they would only try to rationalize that John's risk was minimal. Added to our misgivings was the persistent late night and morning hours involved with his working his way into the drug culture.

Looking at this whole situation in a natural, worldly way, we would have wanted him to drop the "whole ball of wax," and pursue something much safer and more socially acceptable. From a supernatural aspect, we prayed that God was working in John's life and drawing him towards our Lord Jesus, and protecting him from harm. We also felt that drug sales and other satanic evils in our society had to be combated by highly capable, honest men, and that the police force needed the example and strength of true Christians within the department. And so after continual prayer we put John in God's loving hands along with the whole situation.

Shortly thereafter John answered the altar call at the Billy Graham film, "Time to Run," and since then we have seen a tremendous growth in his perception of truth, life and values. There is a new openness as he shares and relates in a much closer way to the rest of us.

There was a little conflict between our daughter Mary and us, although her brothers thought we spoiled her.

At fourteen years of age I began to witness the typical teen-age girl syndrome coming upon Mary. After she attended a Billy Graham Youth Rally I could see a sweetness come over her, but it wasn't until later that she told us she had accepted Jesus as her personal Lord and Saviour. She really became "sweet sixteen" a year later when she was baptized in the Holy Spirit.

Our last son, Mark, is a real gift from God! Before he was born I really understood for the first time with my heart that our children are only loaned to us—they really belong to our Heavenly Father.

Mark, at age four, had a fever seizure with a temperature of 105° and stopped breathing. Again the "test" came without John's presence (he was gone on a five-day around the world trip), my dependence was totally on God again—except this time the other children supported in prayer. I realized how perhaps our little one had become an idol in our eyes, and now was the time that God would take him home. As much as we loved him I knew God loved him even more. It is easier to "let go" when we know God is in full control.

The brain-wave tests produced very erratic readings every time. These indicated that something serious had occurred within that marvelous, unfathomable human computer endowed Mark by his Creator. In order to prevent a recurrent seizure the medication prescribed was to be taken twice daily until he reached puberty. By then he should have outlived and outgrown the danger of added seizures and brain damage. The side effects of the drug made him either over-active or drowsy, depending on the types prescribed. So when faced with such a brick-wall situation, we put him in God's hands and left him there as months passed.

In the midst of a Monday night prayer meeting, Mark, who was then five years old, came and asked for prayers for a sore throat and a cold. As the group prayed we asked our Creator to heal him of everything including the brain condition. God did just that in a beautiful, thorough way.

Mark's next scheduled examination by the neurosurgeon included a brain-wave exam (electro-encephlogram) that read perfectly normal for the first time since the seizure. The specialist could hardly believe it, and had no natural explanation for what had occurred. So we gave him the "supernatural" explanation and he said all medication could be stopped.

As we had left our young son in our Lord's hands completely and patiently, He looked at the whole situation from the viewpoint of all eternity—past, present and future, at all the persons involved in it in any way, relatives, friends, doctors, hospital personnel, prayer group members, and He moved to produce the healing at the best time possible for all concerned. We thank God for *His timing*, not ours because His ways are so far above our ways.

LIFE'S TRAINING GROUND

Frequently, family members will go to a funeral home to see a loved one lying in a casket; and as they stand there and reflect, all too frequently there are thoughts of regret for not having taken time out in life to really share one's true feelings in honest dialogue.

This situation, even though unfortunate, certainly is not necessary if we would each resolve in our hearts to make an extra-special effort at communicating with those who live under the same roof. We seem to find it easier to communicate with those outside the family, rather than with those we are most intimately related.

I believe that it is only as we draw close to Jesus and the Holy Spirit that we can be particularly sensitive in this regard. Many families experience something like a "cold war." Even though they live under the same roof and eat at the same table, and watch the same television set, they have not learned to communicate. By communication I don't simply mean just talking about the weather, politics, or neighborhood gossip— but rather sharing those things which are nearest and dearest to our hearts.

A number of years ago, I was invited to speak at the Somerset County chapter of the Full Gospel Businessmen. Larry Nemanic, one of the officers, acted as my host during the visit. Taking advantage of time we had together, we quickly became buddies in the Lord. Larry, a graduate of St. Francis College in Loretto, has a bachelor's of science in sociology. He is presently a newly-wed of August, 1976, and a field underwriter for the New York Life Insurance Company working out of Johnstown, Pennsylvania.

Larry comes from a large family, and on one occasion invited me to his home for a birthday party. It was certainly a festive event and all of the married brothers and sisters, along with their spouses and children, gathered together around the large dining room table to celebrate the birthday of a younger family member. Frequently, families come together for Christmas and Easter, but this birthday celebration was as beautiful as one of the major holidays. I couldn't help being impressed by the give and take, humor, and exchange of love that was so evident in this family.

Because of this experience, I have asked Larry to share on developing communication among family members.

* * * * *

One of the greatest blessings that the Lord has bestowed upon me is coming from a large family. Because of this, sharing has been a big part of my life, not only because my parents believed in it, but mostly out of necessity.

I can remember how petrified my twin sister, Peg, and I were on our first day of school. Where did all these other children come from? We didn't know there were so many other children in the world. The entire first year Peg and I kept ourselves tied close to the apron strings of our teacher. It took fifteen years for us to get over our shyness, until we became involved in high school activities that excluded our brothers and sisters.

There was one particular incident that challenged and deepened the faith of our family. Mother had a faith in God that was hard to shake and it was this faith that caused her to pray and plead with God to save my brother's life at the age of thirteen.

Michael had lost a good bit of weight in a short period of time which caused us some concern. He began to drink gallons of liquids and urinated excessively until most of the necessary nutrients were drained out of his body. He went into a stupor and very shortly into a coma.

When Dad took him to the hospital, mother went into action. She asked me to call the convent and request prayer and she began to plead and weep before the Lord. It was not long until the phone rang and across the wires came the agonizing report that Michael was near death. The doctors gave him two hours to live. Immediately, things took on a completely different light; we all began to cry, but through those tears in mother's eyes one could sense a peace and a calm about the whole thing. Because of mother's faith in God's healing virtue, Michael is a walking miracle today. Mother understood Matthew 21:22, "And all things, what so ever ye shall ask in prayer, believing, ye shall receive." God is so good! I know that Dad strongly trusted God through this trial. His steady unfaltering acceptance of duty toward Michael and the family is indelibly recorded on the tablet of my heart.

Although the Nemanic family came away from Michael's near-death experience realizing that God was on our side, it was with mixed feelings and uncertainty that I left the warmth of our home to enter college. I was not sure of the future. Four years later after much experimentation in all kinds of college activity, some godly and some very ungodly, I was still searching.

Before I knew it, I was signing up in the Navy Reserve program. I have many pleasant memories about my first navy duty station in Williamsburg, but my soul was starving for something that I could not find.

I was on a ship for two weeks (on a six-month cruise in the Mediterranean) when God revealed Himself to me, filled me with the Holy Spirit and put within me a desire to serve Him with all my heart. At that one moment all the experiences of my childhood, all my religious training, and the faith I saw in my parents suddenly made sense.

I would like to share some of the positive characteristics that I recognized in our family life that fostered good brother-sister relationships.

The quality of brother-sister relationships is in direct proportion to the love that is shown in the home especially between husband and wife. The most favored children in the world are the ones whose parents love each other! The greatest thing I can do for my children is to love their mother well, and it takes a lot of love to raise good children.

I do not want to give the impression that my parents are perfect, because no one is. But in spite of their shortcomings, one thing was always clear to me: they loved each other and in turn loved us children.

In everyday family relationships it is inevitable that each will frequently hurt, and in turn be hurt by others. This is especially true in a family such as ours with eight children. It is absolutely necessary to grow in the ability to absorb the hurt without lashing back; to forgive with such understanding that the loving relationship is quickly reestablished.

I was playing basketball one day and suffered an injury to my ankle. I did not know that it was broken but there was plenty of pain.

"I think we had better take a ride to the hospital just to be sure," exclaimed mother. "We don't want to take any chances."

"I do not think it is necessary," objected Dad. "He will be all right in the morning."

This was not at all typical of Dad, so I began to wonder a little. Dad ended up taking me to the hospital. When we arrived we had to wait, as usual in most hospitals, and I noticed Dad was very quiet, in fact he did not even say a word. This behavior distressed me. At last it was our turn to be treated.

"What is your name?" asked the nurse, and before I could say a word Dad blurted out, "His name is Michael, Michael Anthony."

My Dad stood there and lied on every question, giving the nurse my brother's name and the information on him. It shattered me. How could my father ever do anything like that! Every ounce of respect I had for him just drained out of me.

While in the waiting room I finally mustered up the courage and challenged him.

"Dad," I stammered, "you know what you just did is not right. How could you stand there and lie like that?" Instead I got a surprise.

"You are right, Larry," he answered in a loving way, "I am very sorry. It is just that I do not have any money and you are not covered on my hospital plan, but Michael is." Just as fast as he said that, he grabbed me by the hand and said,"Come on, we have got some straightening out to do." I never respected my father more than on that day. Not only was I able to forgive him for a mistake, but I loved him for admitting his sin and correcting the wrong.

My twin Peg and I had many great joys together, but we've had many instances in which forgiveness and love had to be exercised. One such experience occurred while we were in Spanish class. Each of us had to prepare a short talk in Spanish, and our grade was determined on how well we delivered the speech to the class. The paper on which the speech was written was allowed to be handed to anyone in the first row for prompting, if needed. When it was my turn, I naturally gave mine to good old twinsy. I got about one-fourth of the way through the speech when my mind went blank, and all I could do was look stupid. Peg saw the dumb look on my face and as I looked to her for prompting, she burst into uncontrollable laughter. The rest of the class hesitated, and then they all began to laugh while I turned three shades of red. When I determined that there was to be no prompting from "Sis" that day, I grabbed my paper and read the rest of the speech, verbatim. My grade was so bad and I was so mad I didn't talk to Peg for a week. It took a while, but I finally found forgiveness in my heart.

LIFE UNDER THE COMMANDER IN CHIEF

I particularly delight in ministering to college and university students. Because of this, I greatly look forward to returning to Indiana University of Pennsylvania. Dr. Jack Shepler, a mathematics professor had invited me to come in 1971 to speak to the college students at Graystone United Presbyterian Church for a Sunday night prayer and praise meeting.

Since that time, I have had the opportunity not only to speak at the college and church, but the Full Gospel Business Men's meetings there and enjoy many hours of fellowship with Jack, his wife Gloria and family.

I have always admired and respected Jack in a great way because of the very beautiful reflection and expression of Jesus in his life. Jack is a very masculine and virile individual, and at the same time very tender, gentle and loving. Because of the well-balanced blending of these qualities in Jack's life, and by his example many college students have been edified, and encouraged in their faith and love for the Lord Jesus.

One particular Sunday that I was to speak, I was also scheduled to receive from Jack the manuscript of his chapter for this book. I had arrived at the church just moments before the meeting was to begin and did not have time to talk with Jack at any great length, but I did ask him about the completion of his chapter. He indicated that it wasn't completed even though the deadline date had passed. When I got up to speak I jokingly, yet seriously, remarked to the congregation about this upcoming book and Jack's role in it. I encouraged the body of Christians there to pray, exhort, and encourage Jack to complete his chapter.

At the close of the meeting, I went back to Jack's home to stay overnight. We planned to have some fellowship and discuss the book the next morning after his classes were over. During those hours while I was waiting for Jack to come home, I was praying and was convicted by the Holy Spirit that my remarks the evening before about Jack's tardiness in not having his chapter completed were out of order.

When Jack returned from classes I said, "Jack, I am very sorry for what I said last night to the congregation about you not having the chapter completed and asking them to exhort and pray and encourage you to finish it. Will you forgive me?" With that Jack smiled and said, "Mike, this morning when I went to class I walked in and one of my students said, 'Dr. Shepler, do you have your chapter done yet.' " We both cracked up laughing, exchanging hugs in knowing the Lord's forgiveness, patience, and blessings upon us.

Jack will share some insight and experiences in living under the Lord Jesus Christ, our Commander in Chief.

* * * * *

My first meaningful encounter with Christ took place at the altar of a small Free Methodist Church in Western Pennsylvania. As a nine-year-old I repented of my sins, accepted God's free gift of salvation through Jesus Christ and invited Christ to come into my life. However, it wasn't until twenty-one years later, after much time in the desert of self achievement and bowing down to the idols of education and success, that I truly confessed Jesus Christ as LORD of my life.

Upon graduating from Roberts Wesleyan College I began teaching secondary math in Batavia, New York. It was there that I met my wife. Gloria was a church-goer and I was a rebellious Christian. After several rocky years we packed all our belongings, sold our furniture and moved to San Diego while I worked on a master's degree. There, in a Baptist Church, Gloria responded to an invitation to confess Jesus as her Saviour. Although we now both knew Jesus as our Saviour, we never prayed or studied the Bible together. Christianity was not central in our life style, which had become very materialistically oriented.

Several years later we moved to Madison, Wisconsin, while I studied for my doctorate. In my third year as a graduate student at the Universtiy of Wisconsin, we saw terrible riots caused by a confrontation of students and the National Guard over the Vietnam issue. I finally realized that more education was not the answer to man's problems. Yet Christianity, as my wife and I were living it, was dull and empty.

I accepted a position in the Mathematics Department at Indiana University of Pennsylvania. This brought me in contact with several professors whose lives were vitally alive with Christ's presence. Through their example and witness I seriously began seeking a deeper relationship with God. My many years of determining my own course in life, and the stress of the doctoral program, had taken its toll on me physically. The realization finally dawned that I wasn't smart enough to captain my own ship.

In desperation, on January 25, 1970, I got down on my knees beside my bed and told God I had made a mess of my life and needed new management. I confessed Jesus Christ as LORD OF MY LIFE, turning over to Him all that really belonged to Him anyway, such as my money, my car, my house and my family. This was the source of the problem—everything, including the bills were MINE and therefore I had to worry about them. Rather than thinking of myself as God's

71

steward, managing what He had entrusted to me, I thought of them as mine. Turning these things over to Christ freed me of the cares which had become such a tremendous burden. Two weeks later my wife and I were baptized in the Holy Spirit.

We need Jesus as baptizer to live the abundant Christian life in the nitty-gritty of every-day trials and opportunities here on earth. Yet we need more than a one-time experience in being filled with God's Spirit. Being filled with the Holy Spirit today rests on Jesus being *Lord of our lives* AND on *our obedience to His will.*

We finally came to that place where we are learning that worry and fret over the details of life are sin–doubting God's ability to take care of the situation.

Here are some of the priorities we had to learn:

1. For the husband, his first priority in a love relationship is to his wife. We men should be servant leaders of our wives and die to our own rights and selfish desires.

Besides the love relationship with our wives, our responsibility toward our children is to love and instruct them in the ways of God, and to discipline and counsel them as they grow (Deuteronomy 6:4-6). Fellowship and ministry within the family is of prime importance in God's sight. At one time I was out ministering almost every night of the week. My wife once said, "You have time to minister to everyone except me." It took several years for me to realize that what I was doing was not in God's perfect will.

2. God's second priority is our relationship with our brothers and sisters in Christ. Jesus said, "A new commandment I give to you, that you love one another; even as I have loved you, that you also love one another. By this shall all men know that you are my disciples, if you have love one for another" (John 13:34,35).

3. God's third priority for our lives is to be a witness to the world of God's redeeming love and grace. The Scriptures tell us we are to practice hospitality, take in strangers in need,

and be willing to freely give of ourselves to others.

4. A major priority of God's is for our family to be a witness of His redeeming love. As someone has said, "We need to walk the talk rather than talk the walk." Our children soon see through our hypocrisy. They need to see us reading our Bibles, praying, witnessing, acting in unselfish ways and sharing our concern for others if we expect them to be that way. Our children need to see their dads loving their wives in practical ways, and loving our children by taking an interest in what they do, and by talking and sharing with them so that they can also express love.

As we meaningfully confess Jesus as Lord of our lives, understanding God's priorities for living, and do what God desires us to do, then our families will reflect the Kingdom of God here on earth.

Life under the Lordship of Jesus is the most exciting, challenging, abundant life style possible here on earth.

LORD, WHAT DO YOU EXPECT OF FATHERS?

After spending ten years in college and universities studying, I had reached a point in my academic career where I had become very discouraged and spiritually dry. I thought it would be best if I took a leave from the seminary before going on for final ordination to reevaluate and examine my vocation. During this leave, I taught psychology in a business school in downtown Pittsburgh, Pennsylvania.

My students invited me to a college prayer meeting. The meeting was being held at Carnegie-Mellon University, and students from Shadyside Hospital School of Nursing, the University of Pittsburgh, Duquesne University, and other schools in the Pittsburgh area gathered for the meeting. It was obvious that these students had had a spiritual experience I had not known. They shared in song, fellowship, study of the Scripture, and testimony of all that Jesus was doing for, in, and through them.

Two of the students I met there were Glenn and Carol. Glenn was studying civil engineering at Carnegie-Mellon, and Carol was a student nurse at Shadyside. They were very much in love; but more evident to me was their love for the Lord. They radiated the joy and victory, and the beauty of Christ in everything they said and did during those meetings. They knew that Jesus cared about every detail of their lives—their grades, academic career, marriage plans, social life, and every detail was important to them.

These students realized that there was something amiss in my own heart. However, they never interrogated or attacked me with criticism—they simply loved me. It was because of their personal love, their prayers, their concern for me as an individual that I too experienced the baptism of the Holy Spirit that same summer.

Since then, Glenn and Carol have married and now have three children. My great delight is to visit their home and enjoy their fellowship as we reminisce of those early days when I first met them and encountered the power of the Holy Spirit.

Glenn is presently a registered professional engineer and works for Bethlehem Steel Corporation in Johnstown, Pennsylvania. Carol is a registered nurse, but more importantly, a full-time mother. They worship at the Oakland United Methodist Church in Johnstown.

Glenn has great insight into the Word of God, and yet, at the same time, maintains a very warm and loving heart toward his family and all those whom he meets. Glenn has an awesome awareness of the responsibilities of parenthood and his job as a father to nurture his children in the Christian faith.

* * * * *

GLENN: We'd like to share some of our ideas and experiences regarding the priesthood of the father to encourage others in their family life. (Although I'm going to use the expression that the father is the "priest" of his family, I believe "priest figure" is a more accurate expression. When Jesus died on the cross, the veil in the temple was torn in two as a sign that personal access to God was made possible.

We need no mediator for communion with God. The theme of the priesthood of the father comes from the semblance of the father's role in the family to the priest's role in Israel as found in the Old Testament. The Bible declares that by virtue of Jesus' atoning death, *all* believers are made priests to God.

There's no doubt of the husband's calling and responsibility for his family. The breakdown of God's order in families is that men have lost the vision of His calling to the priesthood.

Sometimes we want to say, "If only Jesus were here with us today, He could do this or He could do that." But Jesus said, when He was telling His disciples of His coming death, that it was expedient for Him to go. He was going to send the Comforter to be with us forever. So, now, Jesus' calling from God has become our own, and as Jesus is a High Priest, and an advocate, so are we; especially fathers in families.

A fundamental biblical principle is that obedience brings blessing from God; conversely, disobedience brings cursing. Men who neglect their calling as priest of the family will immediately rob their family of many blessings. God is good, so He wants to bless the family. There will be daily confirmation that living within God's plan makes for successful family life.

Carol, in your own words, how would you describe a priest?

CAROL: I'd say a priest is a mediator, or a go-between man and God.

GLENN: In the most basic sense, a priest is one who is called by God to minister, one authorized to perform sacred rites. The priest ministers to man by instructing him in ways of living that are pleasing to God.

Originally, all of Israel was chosen for priesthood (Exodus 19:6), but out of fear of being close to God they declined the office. So when Moses received the Law, Aaron and his descendants were ordained as priests. It would be easy to overlook the fact that a person in those days had to be a Jew first before he could become a priest. To be a priest now one has to be in a covenant relationship with God. I Peter 2:9 reads: "But you are a chosen generation, a royal priesthood, a holy nation, a peculiar people; that you should show forth the praises of him who has called you out of darkness into his marvellous life." In Revelation 1:6 John writes: "And hath made us kings and priests unto God and his Father . . . "

The implication for fathers and priests are obvious; they are primarily responsible for the families' relationship to God. This would include the family's worship, reconciliations, fellowship with God and with one another, and the spiritual instruction within the family.

Hebrews 7:25 portrays the high-priestly role of Jesus. His stance is Godward. It indicates the basic way in which a priest presents his people unto God—He always lives to make intercession for them.

Through prayers of intercession, the parent-priest presents his children to God. Here it is important to recognize the spiritual authority which God invests in one called to be a "priest." His prayers have power because God has charged him with certain responsibility. He dare not evade this responsibility through any feelings of false modesty. The primary responsibility rests with the father, then with the mother, should the father be absent from the home. Called to be a priest unto his family, the father must come reverently yet boldly before God, and present each family member before His presence. This role of priestly intercessor requires a disciplined prayer life.

Carol and I had always prayed for our children before they were born.

When either of our daughters becomes ill, I pray for the

child's healing claiming the promises of healing in the Bible. If the children are frightened when they go to bed, this is a perfect time for the father to intercede in behalf of the child and ask God to take away the fear. Perhaps the fear is from spiritual bondage or oppression. The father by faith has authority over the "powers of darkness." Sometimes the child needs just to be loved, comforted and assured of love. So we intercede for their safety, health and God's blessing.

If our children disobey, act disrespectfully, or sometimes if we discern they're harboring an improper attitude, we spank them and then lead them in a prayer of forgiveness and repentance. We then pray that God will restore that close fellowship. Every night Carol and I pray with the children. This is the time when they can express their prayers to God.

Another type of prayer is the prayer of thanksgiving. We give thanks at mealtime, in family worship and singing, and during devotions.

Money is a practical means of expressing gratitude to God. Giving tithes is an obligation ordained by God, and again this should primarily be the husband's responsibility. A father tuned into the promises of God's generosity can benefit his entire family. Ever since Carol and I set up our first family budget, we have set aside one tenth of our gross income for the Lord's work. It wasn't easy for us at first, but the Lord provided. And very early in our married life we found paying the tithe first was best.

CAROL: What about the teaching aspect, as such, as the father's responsibility?

GLENN: Malachi 2:7 (ASV) tells us, "For the lips of a priest should preserve knowledge, and men should seek instruction from his mouth, for he is the messenger of the Lord of hosts." According to Malachi, the priest is a messenger. Every day parents communicate a message to their children whether they're aware of it or not. We teach by precept and behavior. In every dispensation God has ordained that the spiritual life of His people be centered in the home. God has given us the Holy Spirit to help us be effective teachers.

After reading and before prayer, we like to talk. When Daddy talks about how to ask for forgiveness, there's usually a time soon when he has to ask the children for their forgiveness. When the little ones *see* forgiveness they begin to comprehend the spiritual truth in it.

God places upon us, as parents, the responsibility to teach his Words and His ways to our children at home. This responsibility cannot be relegated to some institution—temple, church or Sunday school. Many people are anointed by the Holy Spirit to specifically teach children; but this still doesn't relieve the father of his priestly responsibility.

ME, A FOSTER PARENT?

The Scripture tells us "Be still and know that I am God." Also, the Word says that "those who wait upon the Lord shall renew their strength." One thing that I miss most by being out of the seminary is much of the quiet time for reflection and thought in communing with God in quietness during those academic years in preparation for the ministry. The work of an evangelist is indeed very exciting. The pace keeps you very much on the move and very actively involved with people in the arena of life. Because of this, it is often difficult even when one desires to be still and get away.

To have this need for quiet time adequately met, I thought of perhaps buying a small place in the mountains where I could get away for retreat, renewal, study and prayer. A friend of mine who knew of my interest in this regard, suggested I call or write Ray Nemeth, a contractor, who owns the Mini-Hut Shiloh Ranch. My friend suggested I call upon him to build for me an "A" frame, or a small mountain chalet, that I might use for the purposes of retreat and renewal.

Even though I did not know Ray personally, I wrote to him and told him about myself and my desire to have such a place. He wrote me a very gracious letter and invited me to visit so that he might show me the "mini-huts" that he builds. He stated in his letter that I was most welcome to come and enjoy their hospitality and a time of renewal and refreshing at their ranch.

The moment I drove into Mini-Hut Shiloh Ranch and stepped out of the car I was greeted with a warm and loving embrace by Ray, Doe, and their four children. I was deeply touched by the love and joy that this family exuded in the Lord. Even though they had been married for 21 years, it looked like they were still on their honeymoon. Their home was very spacious and their door was never locked to friends or strangers. There was a constant flow of children, guests, and friends. Yet, when one wanted to be alone, there was enough property and small "huts" on the grounds where one could get away from the flow of fellowship.

As we sat at the dinner table, I asked them about the things the Lord had been doing in their lives. I was also interested in how they knew so many different people since there were so many visiting their home. Ray and his wife, Doe, began to share with me that not only do they have four children of their own, but in the past years they have had the opportunity to be foster parents to ten other children. The love of this couple and their concern for other children who were not as fortunate as their own was most impressive.

* * * * *

Ray and I always loved kids and wanted to work with teens. One day we were asked to take in Paul who came from a broken home, had taken 39 sleeping pills, and was in the hospital. He needed someone to understand him, to love him, to discipline him, and lead him to Jesus Christ.

He accepted Jesus into his heart the first day.

We had many happy memories with Paul. He desperately needed someone to listen to him. Many a night we'd sit in the kitchen after everyone had gone to bed. We'd finish around one or two o'clock some mornings. But he was able to pour out his feelings as I learned more about him. I prayed with him before retiring.

One night our oldest boy Tom, who was then fourteen years old, was in the bathtub. Paul who was sixteen, went outside, got some snow and dropped it on Tom. Tom slipped under the water with a big screech and splash!

We had a lot of fun and plenty of L.S.D. (love, security and discipline). Paul was with us for several months and then moved in with an uncle. He still keeps in touch with us after six years, and still calls us "Mom and Dad number two."

We heard about and were invited to a Christian organization called the Bair Foundation. Bill Bair started the ministry to care for underprivileged, misguided, parentless children and senior citizens.

Bill invited us to his home and we met Marilyn, Bill's wife and his family. They shared with us about the Foundation work. While we were in the dining room, Tom, our son, was talking in the living room to Jeff, a 16-year-old Bair Foundation kid.

The next day Bill called. "Doe," Bill said, "have you and Ray thought any about taking a youngster?"

I said, "Me, a foster parent?"

Bill said, "Well, Jeff seemed to hit it off with Tom, and Tom asked him if he would like to live in the woods so maybe you could pray about it and ask God what you should do!"

When I told Ray, we all gathered to pray and ask the Lord what to do. The Lord impressed all of us to help Jeff.

Bill and Marilyn brought Jeff and we filled out and signed all the necessary papers. I had mixed feelings about signing those papers. Almost like "Once you put your hand to the plow don't turn back." We thought we were going to help Jeff, but little did we realize we also would get taught and helped.

We began to learn deep in our heart the Scripture "Trust in the Lord with all your heart and lean not on your own understanding."

One day Jeff didn't think he wanted to stay with us any longer. He packed his suitcase and at 10 p.m. said, "I'm leaving, I'm not going to stay here any more!"

"If that's what you feel then go!" (This was not the first time Jeff tried to tell us he was leaving.) After he got out the door we all gathered to pray for him. We turned him over to Jesus.

Twenty minutes later there stood Jeff at the door. "There's bears out here, can I come in?"

That trimmed him to a degree, and it gave us a small dose of trust, real trust, what God can do!

One night we went to another Bair Foundation meeting and Bill introduced Sally. Sally was so thin, about 90 pounds. She just made my heart ache. At the close of the meeting Bill asked if anyone wished to pray with someone to feel free to do so. I felt I must go to pray with Sally. She asked Jesus into her heart and life. I was so thrilled.

After the meeting I said, "Marilyn, does Sally belong to anyone yet?"

"I don't know, I'll find out and let you know," she replied.

The next day the phone rang, Geert, the kid's counsellor said, "Doe, last night you made a request to Marilyn about a girl, Sally?"

I said, "Yes, I did."

"Well, Bill and I feel you can have her if you pray about it asking the Lord first."

"All right."

"Call me back with your answer."

I called Ray, our children Amy, Roxanne and Tom, and Jeff together. We prayed and asked God what to do. We all felt a great big "Yes!" I called Geert and gave him our answer.

When he arrived with Sally I saw she wasn't too happy. Immediately I embraced her and said, "Hi, I'm so glad you came. I just love you so much!"

Test number two had just begun. "Trust in the Lord with all your heart and lean not on your own big fat head" (translation by Doe).

Sally cried and cried, "I want to go home." I heard this all day Sunday and part of the next week. On Wednesday I said, "Ray, is it possible for us to go to Clear Creek Park, we can take our camper and pack a supper and some bats, balls and whatever?"

Ray said, "Sounds good."

Tom 15, Jeff 16, Sally 16, Amy 12, Rocky 9, and Scott 6, had a wonderful time playing ball, racing, hiking along the creek where we parked, and Ray and I relaxed and talked. We couldn't get over what God was doing in the foster kids, and in our kids, and in us!

That was the last I ever heard Sally say, "I want to go home."

We had family devotions every morning and every night. It was so beautiful what was happening. Our kids sharing their bedrooms, clothes, mom and dad, and each other and everything they had. "Give and it shall be given unto you; good measure, pressed down and shaken together and running over," we are told in Luke 6:38.

Sally didn't know how to do a lot of things. She didn't know how to cook, wash or wipe dishes, which became one of her favorite jobs. She learned how to make beds and clean a house. Plus personal grooming, bathing, hair care, and how to wash and set her hair. She learned how to walk like a lady and be a lady. Sally loved to please us.

A short time later we were anxiously asking Bill and Geert for another foster teen. Bill said, "What do you want, a boy or girl?"

Ray and I glanced at each other . . . . a girl? "Yes, Bill, a girl."

"Pray about it, God will send the right one."

One day Jim Erb, a counsellor at that time called, "Doe, we've got your girl."

When Elaine walked in she had a strange odor. But we welcomed her with a big hug. Elaine went upstairs with Amy to put her things away.

The boys waited until the girls came back, they wanted to play a game of kick ball. I said, "Jim, what's that strange odor on that girl?"

Jim said, "I don't know."

We found out later the odor was marijuana. Elaine had been involved with drugs.

It was almost Christmas when Elaine came. We did a lot of baking at that time. Elaine had taken food service at school but she wasn't interested. All she'd do was cry. Finally she and Amy were talking about hard-tack candy and taffy. Well, that was the first sign of interest shown by Elaine. "Can we make some, Mom, can we?"

"Well, what do you need?"

Then the hard-tack was underway with four happy girls working diligently. The hard-tack candy was the biggest hit of all, even visitors, that "special Christmas."

We had three extra kids (which now made seven) now, how, oh, how, would we ever be able to afford presents for all of them? We prayed and asked God for help and guidance. God provided "miracles" to buy tape recorders for all the older kids; coats, pajamas, slippers, robes, and dresses for the girls; suits and jackets for the boys.

We invited the Bill Bair family, friends from Youngstown, Ohio, and the Paul Smith's, for Christmas and had a prayer meeting. It was quite an experience for all of us.

The Bair Foundation has been our prayer support for

the past six years, and helped us so much in all our physical and spiritual needs. We grew through these situations and learned that the only way the job gets done is when one is down on one's knees!

Each day everyone had his own household jobs. Ray would take the boys to work with him and teach them many things about carpentry, and whatever he had to do. At home we would clear the table, wash and wipe dishes, sweep, feed the dogs and cats, clean rooms, fold clothes, or whatever needed doing. We worked together as a family ("Many hands make light work" is an old saying but is so true, and the Scripture tells us, "Those who work—eat"). We had many wonderful times together as a family, and we never knew when an emergency case would be staying overnight, and we loved it!

OUR FIRST ARROW

In 1970, I was working as Director of Religious Education in McKeesport. It was my responsibility to coordinate the spiritual education for the parish.

Among other duties I made available to the people, Bible studies, prayer meetings, rap sessions, films, and guest speakers. Frequently outsiders came to the meetings.

One evening a young lady came to me and said, "Brother Mike, is Mr. Richard Gaydos related to you?" "Yes," I responded, "he is my brother." "Oh, he is so handsome and such a fantastic teacher," said Judy. After sharing a bit, this young lady introduced herself as Judy Janeckey.

Since that evening, I watched Judy grow in her love and relationship to the Lord. In the brief years since then, she married Michael Pearce. I had the opportunity to be at their wedding, and I knew that they were very much in love with Jesus and each other, and that their expression of this mutual love would bring forth much fruit in their marriage and in the body of Christ.

Upon the birth of their first "arrow," I expressed my congratulations with the following words by Evelyn Greenway (taken from a Sacred Treasure Card):

Your news is just the greatest
And congratulations go
To quite the proudest parents
That one could ever know.

And although we're data conscious in
this vast computer age,
A baby's something so much more
than weight and lineage.

For God has fashioned each new life
with wise and tender care,
And poured into each tiny frame
Love beyond compare.

And now He has entrusted
this precious one to you,
To train up in HIS glorious way
as only you can do.

In light of all the pressures, uncertainties, anxieties, and fears, that beset many of America's young couples, it gives me great hope to know that there are couples such as Michael and Judy who recognize their joy, privilege and responsibility in bringing forth new life, and are nurturing children in the love and wisdom of the Lord.

* * * * *

"Lo, children are an heritage of the Lord: and the fruit of the womb is his reward. As arrows are in the hand of a mighty man; so are children of the youth. Happy is the man that hath his quiver full of them . . . " (Psalm 127:3-5).

There are various kinds of joy that can be experienced in one's lifetime, and perhaps the greatest joy allowed mankind is the ability to cooperate with God in bringing forth new life. We began discussing this particular joy for ourselves when some close friends of ours had a baby girl.

We had been married almost a year when a trip to the doctor's confirmed that Judy was pregnant with our first child. A tiny, new life was beginning, invisible to the naked eye, but perfectly formed in the eyes of God. "For Thou didst form my inward parts; Thou didst weave me in my mother's womb. I will give thanks to Thee, for I am fearfully and wonderfully made; wonderful are Thy works, and my soul knows it very well. My frame was not hid from Thee, when I was made in secret, and skillfully wrought in the depths of the earth. Thine eyes have seen my unformed substance; and in Thy book they were all written, the days that were ordained for me, when as yet there was not one of them" (Psalm 139:13-16 NAS). We were overwhelmed with joy, yet awed at the responsibility of raising our child in the ways of the Lord.

During Judy's pregnancy, we were surprised at some of the negative comments that people expressed concerning the raising of children in this day and age. The difference between Christian and non-Christian parenthood was readily evident. Environmental pollution, the rising cost of living and the overall uncertainty of facing the future seemed to create fear in people towards raising children. But since we are Christians, the Word shows us that God is bigger than all the problems, and that He is Lord of all. Having a baby is one of the blessings of life, and there is no need to be robbed of the joy that God intended. We believed God for a healthy baby according to His Word.

Our baby girl arrived November 29, 1974. The amazement and wonder of the gift of life that God had shared with us was overwhelming. We praised and thanked God for allowing us this joy. We both were crying and laughing. It was a moment when we realized that we had good and bad times ahead of us. But most important, we had Jesus as Lord to help us through the bad, and rejoice with us in the good.

One situation in which the Lord demonstrated His Lordship occurred a few days following Erin's birth. She developed jaundice, and our pediatrician told us to bring her to his office once a week for six weeks for blood tests. We were both concerned, but put our child's health in the hands of the Lord. Thanks be to God, her jaundice was healed at the end of two weeks, and our faith and trust in the Lord was strengthened.

With a new baby in the house, there was much adjusting to be done. It was difficult getting used to managing on very little sleep. During the first few weeks, it was also very hard to adjust to the added jobs that had to be done to meet the baby's needs. This was the time for me to minister to my wife by helping with the daily chores of housework. It was a time to lay aside the briefcase and pick up a broom.

After Erin's birth, it seemed to Judy that there wasn't enough time to do anything. It was difficult to find time to read the Word, spend time with me, and keep up her appearance the way she would have liked.

Before Erin was born, we had always been able to go out, just the two of us, whenever we felt like it. We were independent. But with the arrival of the new baby, we both realized that the new responsibility greatly limited our freedom. We had to make a special effort to spend time with each other.

At first, we also made the mistake of letting Erin take over our household time. If we were to go somewhere at 1 p.m. and she was asleep, we went late. We look back now and see how ridiculous this was, and how we unnecessarily confined ourselves. Babies adapt to changes very readily. We are not saying one should have no order, but be flexible and ready to flow with each day's occurrences. We have since learned with our second child, Matthew, that children love to go, and are just as happy sleeping on a well-padded floor as they are in their own crib.

During the pregnancy, and the days following the children's birth, I became aware that Judy was undergoing tremendous physical and emotional changes, and I needed to be especially loving and understanding of her moods, and be willing to share the work around the house to relieve her tiredness.

It would be easy to have our life child-centered. However, an imbalance in this area would surely affect the husband-wife relationship . . . a relationship created by God as a symbol of His relationship with the church and we must take care that our relationship with our spouse reflects God's purpose. We recognize that the Lord gave us our children when He did in order to benefit us in our walk with Him, and when they are grown and gone we still want to have a strong husband/wife relationship.

OUT OF THE DEPTHS OF DESPAIR

A warm and inviting fire, hot buttered popcorn, the beautiful sounds of teens singing to a piano, and wall-to-wall love are the ingredients of the Grytness family living room.

However, it was not always that way. They have learned that Jesus is the "joy of living."

J—Jesus, first
O—others second
Y—yourself third

It is all because of Jesus that Dale and Joy Grytness have a remarkable story. I invite you to behold the mercy of God in action as you read the transforming power of the Lord Jesus Christ in this home and family.

Dale has 25 years experience as an accountant, and is now working as a pastor's assistant at the First Baptist Church in Arcata, California. He plans to go to Norway as a missionary in the near future.

Joy has a Masters in Education, and she and Dale have three married children.

* * * * *

Dale and I had been "coke" buddies for the two years

we had been at Washington State College, so it didn't surprise me when he called my sorority house and wanted me to meet him at the "Coug" for a coke.

He has always been direct and to the point, but it did surprise me when he asked as we sipped our cokes:

"I love you . . . will you marry me?"

I didn't say yes until a few months later. We had a happy-go-lucky attitude, with no idea of what marriage could involve. I took his fraternity pin, loving the romance of it all. Dale was 22, and I, 20.

Being the youngest, my family spoiled me, and in love shielded me from every disagreeable situation they could. Their protection was something I came to depend on. Many times my mom did my chores so that I could go to school activities, and things that I wanted to do. I grew up self-centered, with a feeling that I deserved all good things. I felt loved, although love to me was letting me have my own way.

Dale tells this of his early life:

"I had always felt short-changed because I was raised without any brothers or sisters. When asked I would say I had two sisters, but did not tell that they had died before I was born. I remember being lonely and shy. It was difficult for me to relate to other kids at school.

"I learned a work discipline in my father's butcher shop. My mother worked there also. We were a family team. Everyone liked my dad. He was a good butcher and honest and fair with his customers. I always felt best when he was pleased with my work.

"Because I didn't become 18 until May of 1944, I almost missed all the action of the War. My home on the sea was the aircraft carrier Bunker Hill. In June of 1946 I was discharged in Rhode Island."

Dale and I were married Thanksgiving Day, 1948.

Charles Dale was born November 28, 1949. Darrell

Christian was born November 26, 1950.

In 1950, also, Dale started his first job out of college with Simpson Timber Company in Shelton, Washington. We were buying a new home there and our life became busy with the whirl of social life, dances, parties, clubs, and church. Many young couples of our age lived around us, and morning bridge parties were common, with the many little children playing together. It was fun.

Our third child, Cheryl Joy was born March 18, 1953.

Things were good for us, but all was not well. The crowd that we were with dealt only in surface relationships. We didn't know how to handle anything deeper. Dale began playing piano for a dance band, and as the children grew, PTA and school activities became priorities.

Neither of us saw the deep need of the other; nor could we have helped. My need was for a lot of attention, and I turned to others for this. Sin was a part of my life. My heart was crying, my soul was sick.

The year Cheryl entered kindergarten I knew I was mentally ill. I stood in the upstairs window of the children's room thinking, *What a relief it would be to jump.* What I was thinking frightened me. As the days progressed, the depression deepened. November came and the little chores of dinner, cleaning, washing, became jobs of an immense nature. The problems of the children in school, people relationships, would put me into an anxious crying state. Decisions became impossible.

Dale didn't understand any of my feelings, and as I had never shared myself with anyone, I couldn't sort out my own feelings. I wanted to go home—Mother always had been able to help me. One weekend we drove across the state to see my folks on the farm. As we drove in the driveway, I went completely out of my mind.

I remember nothing about the next six weeks. I was told I stayed with my folks, had three shock treatments a week, and my mom took care of Cheryl and me. Dale took the boys home with him. They went to work and school during the weekdays, then came back the 200 miles each weekend.

The doctor diagnosed my case as a result of an early menopause, but now we know that my case was a result of sin and guilt, not living in God's perfect way.

By Christmas I was able to be home with my family in Shelton, but in six months the symptoms were back. My psychiatrist advised that I go to the State Mental Hospital. With a feeling of relief and fear, I admitted myself. Deep inner fear, anxiety, confusion, filled my body. Problems became enormous, and life not worth living. (In Psalm 107:17 God's Word tells us why this is so: "Some were sick through their sinful ways and because of their iniquities suffered affliction . . . and they drew near the gates of death.")

Our home situation was getting worse. The children were reacting to our unstable home, and showing signs of fears and anxiety. This showed up in problems in school. Dale was confused and tired. He did the best he could.

The doctor didn't know when I could leave the hospital, and I was too frightened to want to leave.

In the spring of 1959 Dale came to the hospital and asked for a divorce.

The next weekend I was home for a visit and was determined to find someone to help. I was very nervous as I sat in Reverend Gene Knautz's office, trying to concentrate on what he was saying. I left the office with a wallet-sized card typed on one side:

As long as Joy Grytness is in the will of God
(doing all God expects me to do in trust)
Joy Grytness
Becomes God's responsibility
He will do for me what I cannot do for myself.
(Proverbs 3:5,6; Psalms 37:1-7)

With new confidence I went home to tell Dale I could get well. "Christ wants our home together. Will you go see Rev. Knautz and hear what he has to say?" I asked him.

Dale at this time was an atheist, and his reaction was negative and discouraging. But Rev. Knautz and I had prayed that my home would be healed, and I went back to the State Hospital Sunday evening claiming that promise.

"I'll come see you this week," Dale said as he dropped me off.

That week God showed us His first miracle. Dale accepted Christ as His Saviour! We were going to keep our home together! I went home that weekend.

The going was not easy, living the Christian life was so new to us. All our problems didn't suddenly dissipate, it took time, and it was painful. It was painful for Dale to take on sudden increased maturity; it was difficult for me to be suddenly well emotionally; the kids didn't suddenly become adjusted; we all didn't suddenly relate and communicate well with each other.

We got through the days only because Dale and I were together in our desire to serve the Lord. This opened the channel for the Holy Spirit to work in our lives.

PENTECOSTAL CELEBRATION

It was impressed upon me to contact each person that I lived with and those persons that I am very close to, to share in this book. But at the same time I was directed to be open and sensitive to any new situations or persons I would encounter in the process of writing this book who might have something of importance to share.

Five months after I began this project, I was in Columbus, Ohio, ministering over a brief weekend. During that time, Mr. Brundage, who was to provide the transportation to one of the meetings, invited me to have dinner with him and his family on Sunday afternoon. I accepted the invitation and was warmly received into their home. Not all of the Brundage's five children were able to be with us for dinner.

However, their son Marty was present on that occasion. I had just met Marty when I came into their home that afternoon. I was able to quietly discern that a life had been changed. The fragrance and beauty, loveliness and grace of Jesus beamed from young Marty's face. I joyfully partook of that dinner and fellowship and praised the living God for what He had done in Marty's life as he began to share with me how the Lord revealed Himself.

Marty's a student at Ohio State University and I know

his story will give hope to high school students and parents who struggle with the problems and pressures of the future-shock generation.

* * * * *

My first experience with the power of God came along with my first confession. I felt good and "clean," and close to God as my Father and Jesus as my Saviour. This is what the Protestants call the "salvation" or born-again experience. I can remember my friend and I running and leaping for joy in ecstasy, intoxicated by the love of God.

Soon, however, my love turned cold as hatred and rebellion filled my life. My father, an Air Force Captain, was away on duty most of the time and my mother had to "wear the pants" in the family. Cruel sibling rivalry was a way of life for me and my three brothers. I felt persecuted by my family and prayed that my parents would go to hell. This was done in childish ignorance, but the hatred was vicious and real.

Blaming God for my unhappiness, I cursed Him and dared Him to do something about it. He didn't do anything— Satan did. At age seven my only idea of the devil's role was to bring temptation to steal, lie, or be disobedient, and I never blamed him for the condemnation I felt for rejecting God. I had committed, I believed, a mortal sin: that dastardly, heinous abomination that sent one to hell.

While building up courage for confession, I overheard my brother, three years older, ask this theological question of a Jesuit friend of the family, "What is the worst sin?" He replied, "The unforgivable sin is apostasy, rejecting God, and blasphemy against the Holy Spirit." Why, that was the sin I had committed!

I was a dead duck, doomed to eternal hellfire! For months I lived in stark fear of condemnation. I finally went to confession, but by that time I was deeply scarred and found it difficult to feel forgiven. I began losing hope, and my love for God was replaced by cold fear of judgment. I dreaded the thought of dying. I knew I would go straight to hell.

On the outside I was a normal, well-liked and well-adjusted kid, but on the inside I was dead and cold, cut off from God's love. I was an atheist at the age of ten, but carefully faked my religious obligations of going to Mass, receiving the sacraments, and serving as an altar boy, so that the truth could not be discovered. At age 13 I prayed my last prayer, "God, if you're real, please reveal yourself to me." Not allowing God to respond, I snapped out of what I thought was foolishness. After this experience, I was convinced that God did not exist.

Our family moved often because of my father's job and new schools were hard to adjust to. In the seventh grade I was uprooted for the second time in as many years. I felt depressed and rejected, and turned to vandalism as an outlet.

In the ninth grade I had my first experience with alcohol; in the tenth grade I tried marijuana; in the eleventh grade, speed; in the twelfth grade, other drugs. I had intellectual pride and scored very well in a national test, and could keep high grades with little study, but education was little more than a joke, a game that one had to play along with.

I rejected school, parents and society and quit high school in the middle of the twelfth grade. School was just part of a corrupt establishment system that made self-destructive robots out of human beings.

I was very disillusioned. Hour after hour of listening to rock music instilled the values and ideals of the rock-drug subculture into my receptive mind. The theme was, *The world is committing suicide,* and the only answer is rejection of the establishment's way of doing things and forming a new society with new and better values, ideals, morals, and religions.

I pursued Carl Jung's revolutionary theories of psychology and ancient Indian rituals using mind-altering drugs for spiritual power and enlightenment, as described in the studies of anthropologist Carlos Castaneda.

By now I rejected my atheism and my intellectual, logical, pragmatic approach to life and decided that love, peace and happiness were the only purpose and goal for mankind. However, the painful awareness of my own hang-ups and lack of love caused guilt and frustration. I would take large doses of LSD in an attempt to shake off the chains of my past.

During this time my parents were being set free from fear and worry over me. They found a way to cope with family problems, especially my rebellion, by the power of God as taught in the Catholic Charismatic renewal. They seemed to be more peaceful, but I resented their attempts to turn me on to their religious beliefs. I identified strongly with Jesus' message of love and self-sacrifice but could not accept the idea of a personal God, the deity of Christ, or the Roman Catholic Church.

In my father's zeal to convert his family he offered the use of the family car to bribe my brother and I into attending a pentecostal service. I witnessed people shouting, jumping and being "slain in the spirit." To me, all this was just a vulgar display of gross self-deception and suggestion. I watched with mixed feelings of amusement, pity and disgust. When I'd had enough I walked out despite my father's attempt to restrain me. I wondered what all this had to do with Jesus' Gospel and His beautiful message of love.

The family car was a source of constant trouble. I had always resented my mother's overprotective attitudes and my father's unwillingness to assert himself on my behalf, and his never failing to oppose me when Mom was on my side. He seemed to try to deliberately humiliate me and show me "who's boss" by subjecting me to rules and briefings and interrogations, all the while subject to my mother's "authority," and never restraining her overprotectiveness. When he backed out of his agreement to let me use the car, I felt a flush of uncontrollable anger and saw myself grab a large butcher knife, only to be cornered by Mother saying, "I rebuke you, devil, in the name of Jesus!" Shocked by her boldness, I lost my anger and left the house in Dad's car (without permission) as quickly as possible, only to find the back door wide open when I returned at dawn the next day.

My rebellion increased and I became determined to assert my independence. In the summer of my eighteenth year tension reached a climax when I struck my father. He did not fight back.

I quit, or was fired, from several jobs and tried dealing drugs on a small scale, but was disillusioned by the drug scene where you had to keep your eye on your "buddies," hoping they weren't "narcs" or thieves.

Finally, my parents asked me to leave the house, so I went to live with friends, and later got a factory job and my own apartment.

I was in love with a girl for the first time and felt very free. My life grew more peaceful and I began to be healed of my past experiences. I became intoxicated with just living.

One day on the job I goofed and messed up my machine. I was scared because the first time I did this in the past I almost lost my job. "God," I prayed, (the first time in years) "if you exist and can fix my machine, please do it and in return I will read your Word regularly." Apparently God can't resist such an invitation, for in minutes the machine was operating normally. I was very surprised at this "coincidence."

A few months later the shop went on strike and I found myself with a lot of time on my hands, so I picked up a pocket New Testament my mother had given me which had been collecting dust for months. It seemed strangely unfamiliar in spite of the eleven years of religious education in parochial schools. Scales fell off my eyes and I saw that everything I had been searching for—peace, love, security— was available right here and now from God. I was awestruck by what I read, and sensed God as a power speaking to me personally through the Word. I felt I'd stumbled upon the "treasure hidden in a field." It staggered me to realize that in all my searching for the truth in drugs, occult and philosophy, the truth had been staring me square in the face, yet I had been too stubborn and blind and hate-filled to see it.

I decided to follow my heart instead of my rebelling intellect and went to the Catholic charismatic prayer meeting my parents were regularly attending. A powerful sense of peace and the presence of God seemed to saturate the atmosphere of the gathering. God began to teach me of His simple principle of faith and trust.

I observed that none of the "straight" people in the prayer group ignored me, or disapproved of my intentionally grubby appearance and hair which hadn't seen a barber's clippers in several years. I was accepted and loved. This deeply impressed me.

I longed for the power of the Holy Spirit that had come to the Apostles on Pentecost. I wanted to be completely "full" of God and speak in unknown tongues and receive the power which Jesus had promised to the disciples through the Paraclete, or Holy Spirit. My mother gave me two helpful books, Stephen Clark's *Baptized in The Spirit,* and Robert Frost's *Aglow With The Spirit.*

For weeks I eagerly waited, nothing happend. I would

open my mouth and just start speaking out, but felt silly and discouraged after a few seconds of what I considered gobbledegook. I knew I had received the Holy Spirit because I had met the scriptural conditions—repent and believe (Acts 2:38). I decided to wait on God.

One night as I lay on my bed I asked myself the question, *Why am I waiting for something I already have?* I decided to open my mouth and speak in "tongues." When I spoke out I felt a warm sense of peace and joy as unknown words flowed almost effortlessly out of my mouth. In fact, it seemed so easy, like I'd been doing it all of my life! The baptism in the Holy Spirit gave me a deep sense of wholeness and completeness. From that time forward my sleep was sound and peaceful. Before this I had often had the feeling while falling asleep of being sucked into a world of black unconsciousness by something beyond my control, or I would wake up in the morning or middle of the night and have a difficult time becoming fully conscious.

I felt joyful and free for a few days, but scars from the past remained, and I soon realized that God needed to do a much deeper work of healing and reconciliation within me and between myself and the members of my family so I decided to go back and be reconciled.

I adjusted quickly to being back in a family. Gone were the tension, quarrels, fights and hassles. I felt I was getting to know my parents in a way I have never known them before. I saw them as people with human weaknesses. There were still times when I felt irritated toward one or more family members, but I found it much easier to control my emotions and deal with problems in a rational peaceful way. The power of God's Spirit didn't make me a saint overnight, but I believe it was a key factor in helping me control my emotions and making family life tolerable. I owe much of my spiritual and emotional growth to my weekly prayer group.

God taught me the hard way the importance of submitting important life decisions to the wisdom and discernment of others, who could give me objective opinions, and spare me the danger of independent actions based on emotions and not on wisdom.

When pain and anxiety became unbearable, I would simply throw myself upon the Lord, letting His Spirit comfort and soothe me, and He began teaching me deep truths in His Word about trust and faith in God's protection.

God is helping me minister to my family, and vice versa. We are praying together more often and a sense of family unity is growing among us. As we learn to respect and love each other very deep healings are taking place.

SEVEN-THIRTY IN THE MORNING

Prayer-saturated people get earth-shaking results. Scripture-saturated people get earth-shaking results. Praise-saturated people get earth-shaking results.

I believe that an individual Christian life is a beautiful witness to the world. The family that has it together as a family and seeks God collectively on a regular basis has a greater and more powerful impact upon the community, nation and world.

Prayer is the most perfect form of energy that man can generate. Learning to pray as an individual, or as a family, requires discipline, practice, obedience and faithfulness. This is no easy task in the midst of the hurry and bustle of Twentieth Century living. Even though it is not easy, it is possible; and the fruit of it will serve to make our families truly the light of the world and the salt of the earth.

I meet many people who love Jesus very much and are rejoicing in the fullness and the power of the Holy Spirit in their lives. Among the two most faithful Catholics I have met are A. P. and Pat Guizerix. During my visits to their home in Picayune, Mississippi, I experienced a miracle each morning.

The Word of God records in the Book of Acts

*(2:14-17 LB) these words shouted to the crowd by Peter:
"Listen, all of you, visitors and residents of Jerusalem alike!
Some of you are saying these men are drunk! It isn't true.
It is much too early for that! People don't get drunk at
9 a.m.! No! What you see this morning was predicted centuries ago by the prophet Joel. 'In the last days,' God said,
'I will pour out my Spirit upon all mankind, and your sons
and daughters shall prophesy, and your young men shall
see visions, and your old men dream dreams.' "*

*I invite you to share with me at 7:30 each morning
in the Guizerix home and discover for yourself the miracle
of a family coming together at the dawn of each new day.*

* * * * *

This is the story of many failures, a persistent wife,
tolerant children, a forced husband and the Lord's blessing.

We were like many Christian homes regarding family
devotions. We prayed at the start of most meals and before
going to bed at night. The meal-time prayer was said by the
youngest child who was capable of memorizing the standard
Catholic grace. Each night the small children were escorted
to bed by a parent who required them to kneel and pray.
We parents noticed a problem with the oldest children
(then 12 and 14) who had slipped out of this requirement
and were saying their own short night prayers.

About this time the Charismatic Renewal reached
Picayune, Mississippi, and Mom and Dad felt the need for
a deeper spiritual life. As the local prayer group grew and
started to mature there were several unsuccessful attempts
to organize a youth prayer group. The attempts made the
charismatic parents conscious of the lack of spiritual direction their children were receiving. Pat, my wife suggested
"We should start a family Bible study." From a good Catholic layman the reply was, "What do we know about the

Bible?" Pat said, "You make my point." The subject was dropped for a few weeks.

One Sunday at dinner persistent Pat informed the family that from now on we would have a short Bible reading before the evening meal each day. The project would start the following night with a short reading by Dad and progress through the family by age, so everyone should get his or her passage picked. The reading would be followed by a short discussion as required. This announcement, not cleared with Dad in advance, was met with semi-rebellion by the children and mild surprise at such a "good" idea by "forced father."

In private the parental conversation went something like: "You could have talked it over with me before making such an announcement." "You weren't doing anything about the family devotions, so I figured we had better get started." "I don't see how we will have time for a Bible study before meals, it will be hard to get the children to cooperate." "Well, anyway it's something." This program lasted about four nights and was never re-instituted.

In the ensuing months, several types of family devotions were attempted with varying degrees of success. There was the daily family rosary, the late evening Bible readings, the Sunday discussion of the Mass Scripture readings, and a very short-lived episode that could be entitled "What did the Lord do for you today?"

Finally, I took the initiative when one of the children asked a question about Catholic doctrine that revealed a lack of knowledge about Catholic church law and beliefs. This caused me, a product of twelve years of Catholic education, to get very disturbed. The parental role reversal was astounding. Usually "forced father" began to teach Pre-Vatican II doctrine, while "poor Pat" tried to say that it was "turning them off."

This last fiasco did one good thing, it got me into the

picture. All of this time the Spirit was at work on the spiritually-slow head of the family.

At this time the Lord was dealing with our prayer group concerning family order. There were teachings based on *The Christian Family* by Larry Christenson, which caused us to realize that if marriage is to be as happy as God intended it those biblical passages concerning family order are to be taken literally. The family order to which we refer is clearly stated in Ephesians 5:22-25: "Wives should be submissive to their husbands as if to the Lord because the husband is head of his wife just as Christ is head of his body the church, as well as its saviour. As the church submits to Christ, so wives should submit to their husbands in everything. Husbands, love your wives, as Christ loved the church." The wife's role is no less important than the husband's but it is different.

With regard to our approach to the family devotional, Pat was taking the head of the household role while I was half-heartedly supporting her ideas. None of these ideas worked because they were not in God's order. The arrogant male approach of the Catholic doctrine sessions didn't work because I was depending on myself and my education to carry it through.

It was at this point that the Lord finally got through to Pat that her approach must be through prayer instead of coercion. Although I was unaware of it at the time, Pat managed to turn me and the family prayer time over to the Lord and no longer spoke about it at all. Daily, I was being held up in her prayers, and often at night when I was asleep she would gently lay her hand on my shoulder and pray for me. She told me later that she also began to ask Jesus to give her a more gentle and quiet spirit (I Peter 3:4). Finally, I realized that I could not solve the problem on my own. As a humble head of the house, I asked the Holy Spirit for help.

Every school morning was a hectic rush to finish break-fast, get dressed and go back for forgotten books and home-work. The beginning of our family's day ended amid barking dogs, fighting children, yelling parents and a departure that would get them to school and work with seconds to spare, maybe.

I have always been the obnoxious type that enjoys getting up early in the morning. Since the Lord's ways are not our ways (Isaiah 55:8), it seems that my type usually has a spouse who has trouble getting started in the morning. The chaos of the morning departure was particularly ob-jectionable to me, and my solution has always been to get everyone up earlier and earlier until there would be enough time for a smooth departure. This never was successful, but it seemed to be the only solution.

I finally realized things were getting worse. There didn't seem to be an answer, so I prayed about this problem and asked the Lord for a solution. Jesus honored His promise and gave me an inspiration.

He showed me how both problems could be solved at once. "Let's schedule all chores and preparations to finish at 7:30 a.m. Everyone must stack their books by the front door and be in the living room for prayer by then. After fifteen minutes of prayer we can go to the car and everyone will be on time and relaxed." While we are acting in His will, He is able to guide and help us in all things. The Lord is so willing to smooth our paths.

Although this new system meant getting up fifteen minutes earlier, the children didn't seem to mind. After a few days we parents noticed a peaceful and quiet attitude as we departed the house in our new unhurried fashion. The few objections soon died away as the family became interested in the *Guidepost's* edition of Pearl Buck's *The Story Bible.* Of course, the fifteen-minute time limit makes a book last a long time, especially since we introduce other material and discussions as appropriate.

Now the most feverish time is the five minutes before 7:30 when there is a rush toward the living room amid shouts of, "It's time to pray!" The shouts may be loud and noisy, but they are music to a parent's ears.

The greatest fruit of our family prayer-time is the acceptance of the Lord's presence in our home. Each family member knows He is with us. Jesus Christ and His Word, the Christian life and the church are common topics under our roof. Family discipline, decisions concerning business or play are handled in the light of our understanding of the Scriptures and God's will. Both parents and children have become accustomed to these frequent references to the leadership of Jesus.

It has not always been this way. Shortly after we began our present time and format, the children kept arriving later and later for devotions. Sometimes they made motions to each other or laughed when someone had a testimony or prayer. During these periods of rebellion it is surprising what can be done with prayer and persistence. When a tardy person arrives to find that everyone has been praying for him, it causes embarrassment or a feeling of love, either of which is effective. Tricia and David had a special love for each other and it seems to find expression at the devotional. The ensuing distractions can take the form of snuggling, giggling, pretending to fight over a pillow or stuffed animal, or just making faces. The normal parental reaction would be anger and to separate them. We felt guided by the Lord to gently quiet them each time (for months) but to let them sit together on the couch as they wished. They are still a distraction at times, but their love has grown into a beautiful brother/sister relationship. This has been a wonderful example of: "All things working together for good to them that love God" (Romans 8:28).

External distractions are not uncommon. During the

spring and summer we have birds in our chimney and their chirping was a disturbance until someone thanked God for the beauty of nature. Now they are a reminder of His love. It is hard to understand why our small dog always barks during our devotional. If he is inside he wants to get out, if outside he wants in. Perhaps the Lord has allowed what appears to be a distraction to show us the difference in our children. At first, the children used to fight over who could leave the room for a few minutes to care for the dog. The change has been gradual, but now this has become a chore. Praise the Lord.

Naturally, we have "urgent" phone calls that are a disturbance, but we have prayed for relief and there has been a marked reduction in their frequency. We used to have car-pool riders knocking on the front door before our prayer time ended, but the children have informed their friends of our schedule and this has stopped. We parents found it remarkable that our children would tell their friends that we pray each morning. We know they must be receiving some static from their peers, but we have not heard a complaint.

A family that is in the habit of praying together can expect miracles from the Lord. Tricia, our five-year-old, had her hand badly smashed in a door by Kathy. It was late at night and everyone was tired, there was a dispute and the door was slammed in anger. Naturally, there was a commotion and the fingers were put in ice-water. All six family members were crowded in a small bathroom so it seemed natural to pray for healing of those little fingers. As we prayed, Tricia's screams diminished to sobs, but there was still hurt and we feared real damage. David, then 14, asked Tricia if she had forgiven Kathy for smashing her fingers. Even though Kathy's apologies were profuse and genuine, Tricia's reply was, "Nun-uh" (no). As we listened in amazement, David told her, "You must forgive Kathy before God can heal your hand." We have been taught by the prayer group that when we are unforgiving, we can block the Lord's power.

Still Tricia could not forgive; we then prayed for her to be able to forgive Kathy. Finally, when she was able to forgive Kathy we asked the Lord to heal Tricia's hand. Within twenty minutes of the accident she was asleep and by morning the hand wasn't even stiff or sore.

Children and parents have learned to expect Jesus to intervene in all aspects of our lives.

David was on a Boy Scout camping trip when he felt a need and called upon God. After two days of a five-day hiking trip his pack frame began to bend. If it had broken his trip would have been ruined. He remembered that Jesus is interested in the whole person not just spiritual welfare. If so, then He must want the camping trip to be a success. David prayed for his pack frame to hold out and it did. He was able to give a witness of this fact to others in the expedition.

Because Skipper, then 14 years old, had reached the "prove it to me" rebellious stage, before the devotional started, we parents thought he would be the hardest to handle. The Lord had sent us a disguised blessing by making him particularly disgusted with our noisy and confusing departure for school. He couldn't understand how we were going to "waste" fifteen precious minutes in prayer and get to school on time, but we did.

Four years later, Skipper now admits that besides getting to school on time, he noticed that he didn't get in as many arguments with David and Kathy after the devotional got started. He wasn't yelling at them to get ready for school so the whole day went better.

Sometimes it takes a very peculiar happening to convince a child that prayer time is good.

We are among a few Catholics living in the "Bible belt" of Mississippi. The other Christian churches have large congregations and sponsor social and educational events open to all Christians. Our children attend many of these gatherings with their friends. David was at one of these teen meetings when they began to discuss the biblical King David. Our Catholic children had always been deficient in Bible discussions, but we had just covered this subject in *The Story Bible.* Our David was the only one in the group who could supply the name of King David's rebellious son, Absalom, and tell how his rebellion ended (2 Samuel 18). Needless to say, the class leader was surprised to find that a Catholic reads the Bible, and our son became pleased with the devotional.

During one particularly difficult period, I was led to "bless" the children at night. In Numbers 6:24-26 God tells Moses how the children of Israel are to be blessed by their fathers. This simple prayer, "The Lord bless you and keep you; the Lord make His face shine on you, and be gracious to you; the Lord lift up His countenance on you, and give you peace," is repeated every night at the foot of each bed. Sometimes the children hear the prayer, but they are usually asleep.

At first I felt a little peculiar repeating a blessing four times every night. It seemed like a waste of time and was too tired anyway. But the Lord has honored that blessing many times. We have seen rebellion diminish in our children; we have felt His love and protection resting on them. In times of extreme stress Pat and I have prayed over a sleeping child by the laying on of hands. The Lord has honored these prayers with immediate results. We have seen 103 degrees of fever disappear within an hour. We have seen a child tire of questionable companions. School grades have shown a marked improvement after prayer. Two children who were always quarreling went from tolerance of each other to a deep affection.

These additional prayers are a product of the prayer

atmosphere that has developed because of our family devotional. We parents are trying to place our trust in the Lord, to turn our children over to Him. It is difficult to depend on God to care for our children, but His care is best. It is only through prayer that we can expect to "let go and let God."

This history covers almost four years of seeking the Lord's guidance in bringing our family to a deeper life in the Spirit. All of us must be patient and accept the Lord's blessings in His own good time.

Other families will have to develop their own method for family devotion, but we have described ours as a suggested starting point.

We pray in the living room which has few distractions and reminders of work or play. All family members, and any house guests, are asked to join our family prayer time. We sit in a conversational circle and get quiet for a few seconds. I open with a short prayer of praise and thanksgiving and each person is given time to offer a prayer (sometimes there is just silence). This is the time for any testimony or even a question about theology, or a spiritual problem. If nothing is expressed, someone starts to read from *The Story Bible.* Usually, there is a question or observation about the passage being read. Whenever we arrive at a stopping place or the time is finished, the page is marked for the following day. Everyone stands and joins hands in a circle and it is time for intercessory prayer. We ask for any immediate need: help with a test, guidance in a business decision, healing for a cut or bruise, relief from worry or nervousness; anything, large or small. The devotional is ended with a "Thank you" to Almighty God for granting our requests.

The Lord has answered many of these requests so quickly and exactly that we are continually amazed. It seems that the unity of the family in prayer must be special to Him as it is to us. Jesus promised that "If two of you agree on earth about anything they ask, it will be done for them by my Father in heaven" (Matthew 18:19). Therefore, we are encouraged to pray with a positive attitude when our entire family is present; this is "expectant faith" in the beginning stages. As the children have seen small requests fulfilled, they and we have become encouraged to ask for even greater blessings.

When a child is rebellious, or having a behavioral problem he or she will be silent and not ask for the Lord's help. At first, we parents found it necessary to make their requests for them. Now brothers and sisters have started doing this for each other. The love that is expressed by one child asking that God grant a blessing to a brother or sister is just beautiful. This didn't develop overnight, it has taken years and we parents must still speak out most of the time.

Summers have always been a hard time to maintain a regular schedule for anything, and the prayer time is no exception. As a matter-of-fact, we just simply didn't have a regular time the first summer. The second year we did a little better, but we still were far short of our school time attendance. This year we started well, with fifteen minutes prayer time at 7:30 so I could get to the office by 8. The children gained the concession that they could do chores and eat after prayer time. As you can imagine, the sleepy eyes of those fresh from bed didn't work too well, so breakfast was required before 7:30. This system worked very well with mother finding that it was easier to run the house when breakfast was through at 7:30 and everyone was ready to start the day.

Then the real problems started. Skipper had found a job that required him to leave the house at 6:45 and he was objecting to getting up fifteen minutes earlier than otherwise necessary. Also, the other children and even Mother didn't want to have to get up early enough to eat breakfast with

Skipper and Dad. David was a counselor at a camp in Texas for two months so he was going to be absent for that period. Kathy was at cheerleader camp for a week. Sometimes in the summer we have found ourselves down to Mom, Dad and Tricia for family prayer. The Lord is honoring our effort and we ask that you pray with us for our family devotional and for yours.

THE LOVE CIRCLE

Ring, ring, ring————

"Hello!"

"Hello, Mike, this is Dennis Cummings."

"Oh, Hi, Denny! It is good to hear your voice."

"It has been a while since we have seen each other and I have been thinking about you and wondering how you are doing."

"This is why I called Mike, I have some things I would like to talk to you about. Can we get together?"

"Oh, sure, Denny. I am speaking at the Coffee House on Saturday evening. Why don't you come over, and after the meeting we can spend some time just sharing whatever is on your mind. Would that be okay?"

"Yes, Mike, I will see you there."

After the meeting and ministry on Saturday, Dennis shared what was on his heart. He was dating Marilyn and they were anticipating their engagement. Denny was much burdened during this time that their relationship wasn't developing as well as he wanted it to in the area of their spirituality.

Dennis was concerned that their relationship and life style more resembled that of an unbeliever than a believer in

117

the Lord Jesus; and he felt even though he and Marilyn loved each other very much, it would be good to see one another less in order that they might maintain and guard as their number one priority, their relationship with Jesus. It was at this time that I assured Dennis that sometimes we are not aware of our own growth, and sometimes we are drawing and moving closer to the Lord when it seems to us that we are slipping behind.

I prayed and encouraged him that the Lord would guard their relationship, continuing to lead them by His Holy Spirit in keeping their premarital relationship pure and keep them walking close to the Lord and to one another.

I was privileged when Dennis and Marilyn came to me later and asked if I would preach at their wedding. They said, "Mike, there are people who just come to church to be baptized, married and to be buried. There will probably be people at our wedding that do not know the Lord Jesus. We would like for you to preach a message on personal salvation rather than talking so much about marriage or about us."

I was deeply impressed by this young couple's priorities. I believe that as many priests and ministers stand before two people who are to become one they wonder WHAT CHANCE DOES THIS MARRIAGE HAVE IN LIGHT OF THE ESCALATING DIVORCE RATES IN THE UNITED STATES?

It was with peace and assurance in my heart that I stood before Dennis and Marilyn on their wedding day to preach the Gospel and witness their exchange of vows. I was confident that their future as husband and wife would weather the storm because of their eagerness and desire to "seek first the kingdom of God and His righteousness" during their months of courtship.

After a spiritual experience, whether it be receiving Jesus or the baptism of the Holy Spirit, healing or the joy of a wedding day, Satan is there to destroy, or rob us of our

118

happiness.

I know that you will be inspired by the honesty and the openness of Dennis and Marilyn. You will share their growth, victories, and their values in maturing in Christ and their relationship to each other before and after the exchange of wedding vows.

* * * * *

As we approached the Greater Pittsburgh Airport I began to wonder whether my wife would be waiting to meet me there. For the past nine days I had been on a missionary trip to Guatemala. The purpose was to build homes for the victims of the February 4 quake. Members of my church were among the 38 men who went on this brief journey.

At a prayer meeting God's Spirit ministered to me with this verse from a song: *Freely, freely you have received. Freely, freely give. Go in My name and because you believe, others will know that I live.* With this, I knew I was to be among the men on the trip.

My wife and I loved each other very much, but at the same time there were areas in our relationship that were not in order. Before I left for Guatemala, Marilyn and I prayed together concerning the problem and asked God to use this nine-day period for a work in both of our lives.

In my own prayers I asked God to show me and teach me whatever I needed to learn to bring us into the relationship a married couple should share.

In Guatemala I was busy doing the work that the local missionaries had planned for us. With all that went on, I didn't get much of a chance to miss Marilyn. As the days quickly approached for us to board the jet for home, I began to look forward to seeing my wife once again, and wanted so much just to hold her in my arms.

A tremendous cloud of doubt began to encompass me as

our plane was taxiing into the terminal: I suppose this doubt had built up through many months of marriage and seemed to culminate just then. *Does she love me enough to be at the airport? Is this really important to her? Or, maybe I am just making more out of this than it all deserves,* I thought.

As I walked briskly toward her much emotion began to well up within me. I wrapped my arms around her and then within my spirit I sensed God had performed a miracle in our marriage.

"I have so much to share with you . . . what God has done," she told me.

When Marilyn and I were planning to be married we made a list of all our financial needs that had to be met in order for us to get married. We came up with a staggering figure for us: $500! I was a student at the time with a very small income, and Marilyn was working, but not in a position to save much of her salary. We took our need to the Lord. We were convinced that He wanted us to be married and approached Him with confidence. Matthew 6:33 tells us, "Seek ye first the kingdom of God, and his righteousness . . . and all things shall be added unto you." We had been seeking God's kingdom, and His will for our lives and He more than graciously supplied our need.

As the relationship grows and becomes meaningful, problems, unfortunately, will accompany this commitment.

It was difficult for me to trust in anyone. My inability to trust people was a defense mechanism from past times of disappointment in others. I was dating a girl and we were at a point of considering marriage. I thought I had given much to the relationship in terms of time and love. I discovered I was being used and made a fool of. I was hurt and willing to do almost anything to repay that hurt. That experience made me reluctant to trust in anyone.

How wonderful God is. He was willing to heal all hurt so I could have a sound relationship with Marilyn. According to Psalm 37:1-7 we are told as we submit ourself and our desires for one another to the Lord, Satan and all his thoughts of doubt are cut down like the grass, and the Lord will uphold us with His hand. By an act of my own will, I trusted in the Lord to provide for Marilyn to accept my personal life.

God's grace enables us to trust in our mate. As love blooms and matures and the walls of insecurity begin to crumble, a fortress of love is erected.

Reverend Geoffrey Bingham gives an illustration concerning love. He calls this the "love circuit."

Consider now what happens in a person's life when this circuit is broken between God and ourself through sin, perhaps disobedience, worry or lack of trust in Him. Now there is no way we can effectively minister to each other with love because the love flow is disconnected.

Perfect, lasting love comes only from Almighty God. Although I have the power to love on my own, it is imperfect and not from God himself.

To restore the love circle once it is broken, we must confess to God our sin according to 1 John 1:9: "If we confess our sin, he is faithful and just to forgive us our sins, and to cleanse us from all unrighteousness." When there is sin between you and your mate such as hurt feelings or resentment, the flow is broken.

Unsettled decisions, or resentments in the dating phase of our life, will only provide instability for married life. Christ desires that we have a harmonious life filled with His love.

The relationship between Marilyn and myself is not responsibility free. When trouble comes between the two of us we have the option of two things: we can say to ourselves there are no hurt feelings and then build resentments. Or, stand up to the problem, face it squarely. We feel the best way is to talk it out, if at all possible, and take it to the Lord in prayer.

We have a built-in road to the very presence of God. We can lay our concerns, problems, ambitions, disappointments and frustrations at the feet of Jesus and leave them there expecting Him to set us free.

We cannot compromise with Christ. We must adjust our lives so that He is first. Marilyn and I had experienced this in our dating relationship, and it was a problem that can occur at anytime, to anyone. Many times I had noticed that our relationship had become distant from Jesus and the walk we had built with Him got "sloppy." It became noticeable to us when we began to pass up needed fellowship by making weak excuses.

It is my responsibility as a husband and head of the relationship, to ensure our walk is maintained and healthy. Each time we step out of line there is consolation and forgiveness in Jesus.

To make our marriage work, Marilyn and I must be committed to one another. This has helped me see the need for a deeper commitment to Jesus. Commitment is proved by our actions, especially in times of crisis. Love is expressed by that commitement.

TOGETHERNESS

Among the many pleasant memories I have is going to visit Ken and Janet Ruzich every summer In Libertyville, Illinois. Each visit I had with them Mark and Norma Barnet would come and spend some time with us.

Mark at the time, was a seminary student studying to be an Episcopal priest. I could greatly identify with Mark during that time because it wasn't long before that I myself was a seminary student and I knew some of the discouraging moments of seminary years. Many of the studies were tedious and difficult, and sometimes we were spending much time learning a lot of theological theory but had little opportunity to express and experience these truths.

Each time I would be with Mark I would try to be extra sensitive to the Holy Spirit in my encouraging him in his vocation, and to assure him that the Lord had some very special blessing and ministry ahead for him, and to stick with his studies.

What a special joy it was for me a number of years later when Mark was ordained. His first assignment was in the State of Washington. I was delighted when I received a letter from him inviting me to come and minister at their church. I could hardly wait to get to Washington.

The only free week I had on my schedule was the week

they were scheduled to move. Although they were in the process of moving, their home, hearts, love, joy and hospitality were so abundantly open and full.

Mark and Norma had a very precious baby— in addition to a number of cats! I'm not exactly a Saint Francis, and I don't have a tremendous fondness for cats. On one Sunday evening they took me to St. Luke's in Seattle to minister with Father Dennis Bennett at the vesper's service of praise.

We would be leaving very early and getting back very late. While we were gone I had the door to my bedroom open, and because of the moving process I didn't bother to unpack. I had my luggage open and spread all over the floor. While we were gone their cats went into my bedroom and did their business on my garment bag.

When we came back from the evening service I walked into my room and saw what had happened. I let out one yell and began to laugh hilariously. Mark and Norma couldn't imagine what I was laughing at. They came in and took one look. So I will not soon forget my experience with the Barnets!

The Lord knows how much of a perfectionist I am and He uses these instances and people and situations for what I call Christian "sandpaper." Those things that the Lord uses to rub off some of the rough edges in our lives.

It is always good and healthy to be able to laugh at ourselves. There was a time in my life when I would find that difficult to do, and there was a time too when I would have been very much upset by what the cat had done. But, praise God, we can grow and mature.

* * * * *

Recently Mark was chaplain for ten days at our youth camp. He was gone on a canoe trip down the river with a unit of campers. Shana, our small daughter, and I were visiting

Vera and Patty, the camp cooks, when Addis, the camp nurse, came running up the trail. It took her a moment to catch her breath. She motioned for me to sit down on a log. I was not expecting the news she had for me.

"Mark has been hurt in a canoe accident on the river. He will be okay, but he is in the hospital," she said, and then suggested that we pray together. We asked the Lord to take care of Mark and protect him.

I saw Mark in the hospital a half hour later and he looked dead. His face was waxen, his mouth open, and his eyes were rolled back in his head. I learned his oral temperature had been as low as sixty-seven degrees, and he felt like it when I kissed him on the cheek. Taking his hand, I began praying. I was surprised that the words coming out of my mouth were from a Jewish prayer that was very special to Mark. I didn't realize I knew it. Finally, Mark seemed to sense that someone was with him.

Every few moments, when Mark's body jerked, I'd pray in the Spirit, using the prayer language that God has given me. His body relaxed immediately, and then we'd talk a bit about how grateful we were that he was alive and that the youngsters who had been with him were safe. We were aware of the presence of God.

Mark remained in the hospital two weeks. In trying to retrieve the capsized canoe, he had been crushed between a fallen tree trunk and the canoe which rolled on top of him, pushing him under the water. He suffered a cracked rib, and for a while, the right kidney was bleeding and did not function. After six weeks Mark was allowed to go back to work.

Friends and strangers all over the country were united in prayer for Mark's recovery. It is no surprise to us that when the community of Christ pray in agreement, those prayers are answered. For didn't Jesus say, "Again I say unto you, That if two of you shall agree on earth as touching any thing that they shall ask, it shall be done for them of my

Father which is in heaven" (Matt. 18:19 KJV)? If two or three are a minimum, then hundreds and thousands must be much more than adequate in God's economy! We know from our history and personal experience that deeper strength is available to us as a body than as individuals. The *minyan,* the quorum needed for public prayer in Jewish tradition, also says this.

While we were in college we experienced "body ministry"—the local gathering of believers in Christ Jesus sharing their spiritual and material gifts and talents with each other—when we met nightly in the college dorm. Prayer, agape meals, spiritual gifts, games in the parks, and service projects together, all combined to draw us together into a unit of Christ's love.

The kind of "body life" we experienced in prayer groups was great! But the scriptures lead us to an even deeper model. In some areas we have lost the balance that belongs to the temple/synagogue/home system.

Jesus was not born in a synagogue congregation. He was born and raised within the family structure. The majority of his religious education and spiritual development took place in the home, just as it did for any Jewish boy or girl. The synagogue is primarily a house of prayer, and secondly a place for instruction. This tradition has been carried over into our churches where many congregations see their life together as one focused on worship and prayer.

How do we, in today's world, make our *families* the center of Christianity?

Many demands are continually placed on us to do this, attend that meeting, help with this project, *et cetera.* We have found it helpful to set some limits on time away from our family. If we find that we have over extended ourselves, we haven't been listening to God's plan for our time. This concept has given us a new freedom from guilt when we say "No" to a proposed activity, no matter how important it may seem to be. After seeking the Lord's will in each situation, we try to compare calendars to ensure that we have enough time together as a family. Part of this time may include other families who have children the same age as Shana. Such times enable us to share what Christ is doing with us as a family, and not just as individuals.

Family devotions have been difficult for us to schedule at a specific hour of the day. Meal time, especially in the evenings, has become a time of sharing what we have learned from our individual devotional readings during the day, or from the experiences we have had. The family supper table, then, acts for us in a very real sense as an altar where we feast on spiritual food as well as physical. At times, we have chosen a specific topic for study and thought during the day.

In addition to our regular times of prayer at meals and in the evening, we have found that praying for a need or praising God as situations arise, has made us more dependent upon each other's ministry. It is almost impossible for us to fake our level of spiritual maturity before our family. Perhaps this is why our family ties are strengthened in this act of submitting to each other.

WHEN SILENCE IS GOLDEN

In the Book of I Samuel 18:1-4, the Scripture tells us that "David met Jonathan, the king's son. There was an immediate bond of love between them. Jonathan swore to be his blood brother and sealed the pact by giving David his robe, sword, bow and belt."

One evening I was exhausted, yet I was scheduled to speak at a prayer meeting for teen-agers. I went to the meeting obedient to the Lord, rather than because of a real desire due to my weariness. I sat there waiting to be introduced thinking, "Lord, how can I ever minister to these young people this evening?" I felt it would be impossible to effectively preach the Word, pray with them, listen to their problems and finally just rap when I would rather be home in bed.

While these thoughts were going through my mind, a young fellow got up and began to lead the group in worship. In his early twenties, he had a guitar in his hand, a smile on his face, a gleam in his eyes, an anointing of the Holy Spirit, a rapport with the kids, and a song in his heart.

The more he sang, the more refreshed I became in the Spirit. He kept singing and I kept rejoicing as all the exhaustion and weariness left my body, and I again experienced the power and anointing of the Holy Spirit. Before he finished singing, I could hardly wait to stand to my feet and begin sharing the Gospel.

After the meeting concluded, I made my way to the brother who had led the music. Although I had never met him before, I approached him by saying, "I was really ministered to by your music this evening, and if you would like, I would enjoy getting together for some tennis, golf, or whatever you would most enjoy." He replied, "Sure, Mike, anytime that is convenient for you, let me know."

The following week as we got together for some recreation and fellowship, Rick and I began to share our lives and experiences and mutual love of the Lord. Rick shared with me that he was a biology teacher, a coach at the Franklin School District, and that he was a graduate student at Indiana University of Pennsylvania.

It amazes me how the Lord can bring two people together with two diverse backgrounds and blend their lives in a deep and intimate friendship. As David met Jonathan, the king's son, there was an immediate bond of love between them. So, too, when I met Rick, there was an immediate bond of love between us. Being raised Catholic, I was never particularly close to Protestants, and especially Baptists; and the subject I disliked most in high school, college and seminary was biology. Yet with such opposite interests, Rick and I became very close brothers in the Lord.

A friend is one who knows you as you are, understands where you have been, accepts who you have become, and still, gently invites you to grow. Rick and I, in our many hours of being together have come to know one another—our sins and failures, as well as our successes and virtues in the Lord; and with all of this, we accept one another and continue to invite each other to grow. I know that you will come to love Rick as I have, as this graduate of Bucknell University shares with you what he has learned in the art of communication.

* * * * *

Our marriage vows before the Lord finalized our commitment to one another. When we were pronounced husband and wife we knew only death would free us from the promises we made. We promised to love, honor, cherish and serve one another for the rest of our lives.

During the adjustment period of our first year of marriage, there were many occasions when we were eyeball to eyeball about our rights as individuals, finances, responsibilities as husband and wife, etc., etc., and etc. Some of our warm discussions rose to a simmer and eventually to a rolling boil as we added fuel to the fire. Many times we said words we later regretted, but through it all we knew we were to cleave to one another. Sooner or later we would have to straighten things out. As our marriage approached its first anniversary, we knew from experience soon was much better than later.

At times, Patty and I are extremely strong-willed individuals. I want to do something, so I do it regardless of her feelings. After all, self preservation of one's personality is a basic right is it not? Both of us took many hard knocks before we realized how wrong this philosophy was. We have understood this for some time now, but it was not until recently we could put it into words. Our individuality is expressed *through* our marriage, not *in spite of* it. Patty's interest in the arts and mine in the natural sciences have brought about a unique enjoyment and understanding of new and exciting areas we never were inclined to explore before. Through the eyes of my spouse, totally new dimensions are waiting for me if I am willing to set aside my desire to please myself first.

Common interests even take on new vistas when we

develop them together. Among the many we have are making things for our apartment, taking walks, growing plants, discussing God's Word, and keeping physically fit. Patty is involved with an exercise program which not only keeps her physically fit, but also maintains her reign as the Miss Universe in my life. My involvement as cross-country and track coach at the high school where I teach leads me into a different program of conditioning. I enjoy running the back roads of Murrysville with the teen-agers I coach while Patty conditions in the home. Although this common interest is expressed predominantly as individuals, the additive effect it has on our marriage is well worth the time we spend apart.

The most precious moments of every day are those which occur immediately after awaking and before retiring. We seldom feel as though we spend enough time together during the course of the day because our responsibilities with our jobs, coaching, housework, education, and even Bible studies preempts time we should be taking to simply enjoy one another. One author knew exactly what the problem was when he stated we were caught in the "tyranny of the urgent." Although Patty and I understood those circumstances which are urgent are not necessarily those which are important, too often we slipped into the snare of occupying our time with the former. Frustration then began to sneak its ugly presence into our relationship.

Those few moments together and with the Lord at the beginning and close of each day are essential. After waking, and before our minds become preoccupied with the schedule of the day, what a joy it is to share our love for one another.

Without a doubt, one of the most devastating ways which we can inflict pain on our spouse is by not accepting their expressions of individuality. The results usually lead to repression or rebellion. In both cases, the partner is forced to look outside marriage for approval and praise.

Being, I guess, a typically jealous husband, I bristle when some members of my sex lavish compliments on Patty. There are those individuals whom I know are sincere and well-meaning with their kind words, and I am flattered as much as Patty. But there are those who by their attitude and words pose a threat to our relationship. I never doubt the integrity of Patty's commitment to our marriage, but nevertheless I experience feelings of competition. This is always a warning signal to me. Questions repeatedly flash through my brain. "Are you demonstrating to Patty both in word and in deed that to you she is the most desirable, lovable, woman in all the world?" "How many times have you told her how much you love her today?" "Have you complimented her on her hair, clothing, the way she walks and her cooking?" "How many times have you held her in your arms and kissed her today?" If I can satisfactorily answer each question in the plural form the doubts I could have harbored about our relationship are immediately dismissed because they lack substance.

An important aspect of all communication is the art of being a good listener. What is the point of Patty attempting to express herself if my mind is lost in my own thoughts, or if she knows I will interrupt with a dissertation every time she stops to inhale, or worst of all, remain engrossed in the Monday-night football game? I have many bad habits in this area. During some of our conversations I begin to perceive frustration building up within her simply because I will not discipline my tongue to remain still until she has finished. I have to make a concerted effort to remain quiet.

Listening can take on many forms. It is the ability to receive, gracefully, some form of communication offered by your spouse. It may even be in the form of a compliment. If your wife admires your physique and says so, accept it. If she places her arm around you or squeezes your hand, even if it is in public, accept her. Edify one another by listening!

It is very difficult to understand how two people manage to fall in love, eventually marry, and then spend most of their lives not touching one another. It never ceases to amaze us the healing that takes place in a single touch. Patty and I discovered this early in our relationship and vowed to one another we would never withhold the physical expression of our love.

Individual quiet times are important for individual growth, but reading Scriptures together will edify and mature our roles as husband and wife. By setting time aside, we are giving God the opportunity to speak to us on topics concerning our relationship to Him as husband and wife, to one another, and to our ministry with our family, friends, and neighbors. Without these directives, and obedience to them, we believe our relationship would run the identical path of many marriages in the country today. Without God, marriage is meaningless.

It is love that cements our relationship with God and with each other. As the author of love, God produces the fruits of love, patience, unselfishness, humility, a realistic appraisal of oneself and others, discipline, truth, endurance through all things, kindness (I Corinthians 13:4-7), responsibility (II Corinthians 5:14-15), forgiveness (I Peter 4:8, Proverbs 13:8a). Patty and I understand we could never hope to produce this type of fruit in our relationship. We are of secondary importance. We need a source—the true vine, Jesus Christ. He produces the fruit. In ourselves, we can no more manufacture the fruits of love than the branch of a grapevine that has been pruned from its source of nourishment.

For our marriage to grow, our relationship with Jesus must have top priority—on an individual basis and as husband and wife. As we pray for the needs of others we know His head is turned in our direction and is eager to hear and answer our petitions.

133

Not only is it important to spend time together in prayer and sharing the Word, but also in fellowship with other Christians. The author of Hebrews 10:25 exhorts us not to forsake assembling together.

YOU FILLED OUR HEARTS

During my seminary years, I spent most of my summers working at camps both in New York and Massachusetts. While serving as a camp counselor at St. Patrick's Military Academy, I ate most of my meals with the school chaplain. One evening he shared with me a burden that was on his heart. He told me of a young fellow by the name of Tommy Decerbo who had attended the academy and had just recently been killed in a very serious automobile accident. He spoke of his attempts to console Tommy's parents.

I was introduced to Mr. and Mrs. Decerbo and it was love at first sight. They needed a son and I needed some parents since I was so far away from home during my seminary years in Connecticut and summers working in New York and Massachussets.

During my short vacations such as Thanksgiving and free weekends, it was impossible for me to travel all the way home to Pennsylvania to visit my beloved dad and mom, but yet it was close enough for me to go to New York. Tom and Olga assured me that their home and heart were open anytime that I cared to visit them. I was very eager and looked forward to each of our visits together. We enjoyed many pleasant experiences in the city, seeing the sights, going to

135

the theater, and having delicious dinners at many of New York's finest restaurants. I always went back to the seminary feeling blessed by the hospitality and generosity of the Decerbos.

One day I received a letter from them telling me that it was always their custom to go to the Virgin Islands during the Easter season and take Tommy with them. Because of their loss, they wanted to take me with them to the islands as their guest. Can you imagine the joy that was mine with such an invitation! Here I was a young seminarian, with very little money and the Lord was giving me an all-expense-paid vacation through these two people. Wow!

This was to be my first long distance trip by plane. As a student, I couldn't afford the plane fare so I would travel from Connecticut to Pennsylvania by bus. Little did I realize then that after I would finish my formal education, the Lord would call me into a world-wide ministry of evangelism.

Our time together in the Virgin Islands was a most memorable experience for me. We only had one week for Easter vacation and I wanted to get the most out of this trip together. I would get up very early in the morning and take long walks on the beach praying, and thanking the Lord for the trip and asking Him to bless Tom and Olga, and to fill their lives with His love and His presence in the loss of their son. I would also stay up very late at night, thinking that if I would get up early and stay up until late, the vacation would seem twice as long and I could make the most of it.

It has been a joy to me down through the years to observe what the Lord is doing in the lives of this beautiful couple, and how He has been drawing them close unto Himself.

* * * * *

The good Lord blessed me with a saintly mother who did not permit or practice gambling. As a result I do not feel that the word "WHY" was ever in my vocabulary. And the teachings in the parochial schools certainly prepared me for the unexpected whereby I gained acceptance of reverses throughout my life.

After a childless marriage of seven years, I had a six-month miscarriage. Then the Lord sent us our Tommy. I told Jesus, "He's yours, Lord, and you direct him to serve you in whatever your plans are and I'll accept, and I place him on your altar."

When Tommy had just celebrated his sixteenth birthday, two weeks later there was an accident and he was killed instantly by a speeding car. At such a time one recalls the designs and plans anticipated for a loved one.

I remembered when Tommy was five years old and he had a special playmate, Barbara Small, and through the children we parents became acquainted. Having experienced the war in Germany, Mrs. Small delayed passing on her religious faith to her children. She had many scars to heal. One day after she had received a letter from her mother in Germany (who reminded her frequently of her religious obligation), she approached me saying that she had consulted with her children about religious services and through Tommy's influence, Barbara (bless her) was inspired to join a church. Consequently the girls, Barbara and Jeanette, were both baptized and confirmed. My husband and I were their sponsors. The children were seven and eleven, and their brother Peter came later and ceremonies for him followed. The Lord was carrying out His plans, and Tommy was his instrument.

We were very much pleasured at another time to hear our son defend his faith when he was challenged at the age of fourteen. As a freshman he was approached by some seniors to come into the discussion of Jesus coming into the world and dying on the cross for us. Tommy said, "I told it all just how I had been taught." When his father expressed the fact that inasmuch as it was an older group it might not have been wise to enter into the discussion of either religion or politics, Tommy proudly answered, "When I made my confirmation I promised to defend my faith and this was my opportunity." (Was I ever proud!) His father then agreed and said, "Good goings, son."

Still another time he defended a little colored boy who was being bullied by some bruisers.

God certainly took over in many instances in his life, so Tommy really exposed himself to many codes. So to be taken so young I had to think he was very special to Jesus to have his life interrupted when we thought it was just beginning.

I thank God daily for having Tommy even for so short a time. I received the necessary graces when I prayed so deeply, and will continue to do so the rest of my days. We too were His chosen.

Evangelist Michael Gaydos

Michael Gaydos

Michael was born in Swissvale, Pennsylvania in 1940. He was baptized at St. Anselm's Church and has loved Jesus and desired to serve him since his youth. Like the Prophet Jeremiah, he realized the Lord's call upon his life at the age of six for the ministry. In 1950, Michael moved with his family to Level Green, Pa. At that time he was confirmed at St. Regis Parish in the Diocese of Greensburg and continues to be a faithful and active member of this congregation. In 1969, Michael was formally set apart for the ministry as a Cleric in the Church by Bishop John King Mussio of the Diocese of Steubenville, Ohio. Because of a serious eye handicap as a baby, he never participated in athletics. Since Mike's healing in 1970, he enthusiastically enjoys skiing, golf and tennis. He delights in praising the Lord and sharing the reality of Jesus with others on the ski slopes. His special interests are music, art and photography.

Academic Profile

After receiving his Cum Laude degree in Business Administration from Robert Morris College, Michael studied liberal arts at Duquesne University in Pittsburgh, Pa. He has also done Biblical and language studies at the University of Steubenville and John Carroll University. At Holy Apostles Seminary in Cromwell, Connecticut and Saint John Vianney Seminary in Bloomingdale, Ohio he majored in philosophy and theology in preparation for the ministry. Michael is a graduate of the Institute of Ministry in Bradenton, Florida. His professional background includes teaching both elementary and secondary grades in parochial schools and serving as Director of Religious Education. Michael has worked with the Jesuits at the Cranwell School in Massachusetts in youth ministry. He has also taught psychology, public speaking, and marketing at the Berkeley School in Pittsburgh.

Books and Media

"Eyes To Behold Him" was published by New Leaf Press and is the testimony of Michael's healing of the eyes at the age of thirty. As he shares with others what the Lord has done for him and preaches the Gospel, the Lord confirms His work by healing the eyes of those who act in faith on the message. "All In A Family" is an inspiring work on the healing and restoration of today's marriages and homes. The author shares much of what he has observed and learned about America's contemporary family life through ministry, study and extended travels. Articles have been published by Michael in periodicals such as Christian Life Magazine and The Catholic Evangelist. "On The Road" is a color film on the renewal in the Church. Michael's ministry of joy and love has inspired the hearts of thousands around the world, as portrayed in the film. Your faith will be challenged and deepened as you read his books and hear him preach and teach Biblical truth.

Visionary Ministries

Michael is the President of Visionary Ministries, with offices in Level Green, Pa., Minneapolis, Minnesota, and Edgewater, Maryland. As an evangelist, Michael travels internationally proclaiming the Good News of the Risen Lord in Catholic and Protestant churches. He has ministered the Word of God at conventions, seminars, college and university campuses, prisons, and on television and radio from coast to coast in the United States and Canada. Michael also has a special compassion and ministry for the depressed and those suffering from stress and burnout. He truly believes that the Lord has come to give us abundantly full life in Christ, and is a faithful instrument in the Lord's hand to impart blessings and healings to others.

Eyes To Behold Him

A fantastic portrayal of God's love and healing...EYES TO BEHOLD HIM is so well orchestrated that it could conceivably carry the subtitle OPUS in SEE SHARP. *Dr. Marvin R. Halgren, Optometrist, Robbinsdale, Minn.*

I have personally known Michael for fifteen years, during which time I have laughed, cried and prayed with him. He has a heart that pants after God. His book will bring blessings and healings to the multitudes who read it. *Cliff Dudley, Author and Publisher*

The joy of the Spirit pervades Michael's very presence and gently opens his message of LOVE to his readers; indeed to the world. His influence has been far-reaching and effective. *Sister Rosemary Yost, OSB*

This book testifies to the great work God is doing in our day. The Lord uses the weak of the world to confound the proud. This autobiography witnesses to God's choosing one of these little ones to show forth His power. *Fr. Michael Scanlan, T.O.R., The University Of Steubenville, Ohio*

Micahel's story of maturing in the Spirit is instructive and inspirational. Under the anointing of the Holy Spirit, he is an evangelist working to renew the temporal order of society and doing works of mercy and charity...especially through his gift of healing. *Reverend Henry R. O'Meara, C.S.S.R. Washington, D.C.*

The times Michael had been with us to worship and preach have deeply touched the lives of our congregation. He works well in a variety of settings and is respectful of the various traditions within the Christian community. *Reverend Michael Bye, Vicar, St. Andrews The Fisherman Church*

Michael has a deep faith in the healing power of the Lord and through that faith wondrous deeds are worked. I am glad we have Michael active in this ministry to make people more aware of the healing power that lies at the heart of our Christian faith. *Reverend Robert Voight, Our Lady of Mount Carmel, Opole, Minn.*

All In A Family

In today's world the family is indeed very fragile. This book helps put family life in perspective; with God as our first priority the rest of our lives fall better into place. Thank you, Michael, for sharing these 'real life struggles' with us. *Marilyn and Frank Klanica, Level Green, Pennsylvania*

ALL IN A FAMILY presents an inspiring account that the Lord deepens the bonds of marriage and family life as He promised the Children of Israel. In this narrative of the contemporary family, Christian theology and scripture are authenticated. Michael has woven a network of interfaith relationships in unifying the Body of Christ. The accounts in this book give witness to the biblical truth that whoever asks shall receive. *Dennis and Rhonda Hagler, Shadyside, Pennsylvania*

Personal Endorsements

Having known Michael for thirty-five years, I have seen a great transformation in Him. The Lord has graciously given him a ministry to the whole man...body, soul and spirit. Under the anointing of the Holy Spirit the Lord uses Michael to set people free from the bondages of depression. He also has heartfelt compassion and understanding in counseling the American family living in the complexity of the twentieth century. *Tony Istanish, Pittsburgh, Pennsylvania*

I first met Michael in the sixth grade. During those years he struggled not only with his physical disability of partial blindness, but also with the emotional trauma of not being accepted by his peers. After enduring this pain for many years the Lord not only filled him to overflowing with His Holy Spirit but healed his physical and emotional problems as well. Michael's life and ministry are a unique witness to the Lord's grace. Michael's walk in the Spirit has been a source of strength and encouragement to me in my Christian life. *Joseph Robinson, Indianapolis, Indiana*

A Personal Endorsement

I have personally known Michael since meeting him at a Bible study on the campus of Carnegie Mellon University in Oakland, Pennsylvania in 1969. During the following eighteen years of his full time ministry we have been in regular fellowship. I can attest to Michael's gifts and motivation for the ministry as an evangelist. In public services, the anointing of the Holy Spirit he has for the proclamation of the Word of God and the miraculous signs of healing is a matter of public record. More importantly, another attestation of Christ's call on his life is his character, love, sound doctrine and steadfastness in a faith ministry. Here in Colorado he is fondly known by skiers as the Chaplain Of The Slopes. *Glenn A. Gilbert, Council Member, Evangelical Covenant Church of Fort Collins*

I have known Michael for seventeen years, and have watched God do mighty miracles thru his ministry, I am thinking about the many remarkable eye healings that follow his testimony and preaching of God's Word. Michael has established lasting friendships across the nation during these years. He has spent innumberable days and nights in Christian homes. His book, ALL IN THE FAMILY has grown out of some of these relationships. Even after these many years, I still remain amazed when I see the results of Michael's ministry. *Russell Bixler, Cornerstone TeleVision, Inc.*

You may contact Evangelist Michael Gaydos by writing him in care of:

VISIONARY MINISTRIES
P.O. Box PTL
Loveland, CO 80539-1733
Telephone: 303-223-7784